Supporting Teachers As Learners

A guide for mentors and coaches
in early care and education

Table of Contents

E arly childhood educators bring a wealth of experiences and knowledge to their learning settings whether they teach in a public pre-K or Head Start classroom, a family child care home or a community-based center. As a profession, educators for centuries have benefited from sharing their best practices, ideas and resources. Peer-to-peer learning and professional growth happen when educators have genuine opportunities to meet and discuss common challenges.

In *Supporting Teachers as Learners: A Guide for Mentors and Coaches in Early Care and Education*, Marcy Whitebook and Dan Bellm have produced a resource that guides early childhood educators through their mentoring partnerships. Whether this mentoring is formal or informal, spans years or weeks, the ideas and strategies developed by Marcy and Dan offer an invaluable framework. They provide unique plans, strategies and discussion questions—tools that can be adapted to serve the needs of nearly any mentoring partnership. As one of our members, who has mentored fellow teachers both formally and informally for more than 15 years, said, "I wish I had this book when I first started mentoring!" At the AFT, we believe that educators are strongest when we stand together. For this reason, it is our honor to offer you *Supporting Teachers as Learners*.

For far too long, the needs of our youngest learners and the educators who work with them have been neglected. Yet with each passing year, the evidence becomes undeniable as to how vital the years before kindergarten are in a child's development and how far high-quality early learning opportunities can go in helping children succeed in the long run. Even when school budgets are austere, or just tight, we will continue to fight for the resources our youngest learners need to truly benefit from their early learning programs. Mentoring between early childhood educators—whether it is a veteran teacher generating new ways to present a familiar topic to her students or a new teacher developing classroom management strategies—will foster best practices and enable educators to meet their professional goals.

Marcy and Dan understand that meaningful exchanges between educators facilitate the type of continual professional growth that allows them to share knowledge, challenges, ideas and support and to build on skills that ultimately lead to the high-quality early learning every child deserves. This simple premise is the foundation of *Supporting Teachers as Learners*.

I extend my heartfelt thanks for all you do for our youngest learners and trust that this book will serve you well as you mentor, coach and learn from your fellow early childhood educators.

Randi Weingarten, President
American Federation of Teachers

In the field of early care and education (ECE), mentoring is a relationship-based arrangement designed to facilitate the learning and professional development of teachers or other practitioners.[1] Teachers face increasing standards and expectations about what they should know and be able to do in promoting children's early learning and development, and this has led to a dramatic surge in the types and numbers of mentoring opportunities operating within the ECE field. Particularly in public school classrooms, mentoring may be a required part of one's first year of teaching. With the recent rise in higher education requirements for teachers in Head Start and many publicly funded pre-K programs, along with the emergence of quality rating and improvement systems (QRIS) in many states, protégés—i.e., teachers working with a mentor—are now just as likely to be experienced teachers as to be novices to the profession. These changes have brought about many new mentoring and other professional development roles.

Mentors may work in their own classrooms, or in their protégés' classrooms or family child care homes. Many have worked as classroom teachers or home-based providers themselves, but a sizable proportion have not. Some mentors have considerable autonomy in determining the focus and content of their relationship with protégés, while others are expected to help protégés learn a particular curriculum model or work on a specific skill. Mentoring efforts can also vary widely in time frame, from a matter of weeks or months to a year or more.

The proliferating variety of mentoring programs underscores the need for clearer definitions and terminology about these different professional development arrangements, as well as greater awareness of the challenges and benefits of each approach. Equally needed are more clearly articulated competencies for mentors that emphasize the importance of foundational teaching experience; sound knowledge of pedagogy with young children; training related to understanding and facilitating adult learning; respect for protégés' perspective and skills; and sensitivity to the dynamics of the mentor-protégé relationship and the context in which it occurs.

Because of such changes in the ECE field over the last two decades, the time is right for a completely new version of our *Early Childhood Mentoring Curriculum*, first published in 1997, that can reflect the changing mentoring terrain and the multiple contexts in which mentoring now takes place. This book is intended for all who are working in mentoring or other roles to educate and support teachers and family child care providers in their practice with children. It can serve as the text for a training series or credit-bearing course on mentoring, and can also be used by anyone involved in providing professional development to teachers and other practitioners in a variety of ECE settings.

---

1. While this book addresses formalized mentoring relationships, mentoring can also happen more informally in early care and education programs—for example, as a director seeks to guide a teacher's development and practice, or as a teacher works with paraprofessionals or other assistants in the classroom. Note, however—as discussed in more detail in Chapter 3 —that mentoring is *not* the same as supervision.

Throughout this book, you will find suggestions for journal writing, questions for discussion, and other activities interspersed in the text. These can be adapted for use in a mentor training group or course, on your own or in working with protégés. The activities are intended to:

- Help you as a mentor to identify and reflect on your skills, perspectives, strengths and challenges as a teacher of young children and as a mentor to other adults;
- Build your awareness of the context that shapes mentor-protégé relationships, including adult development, adult learning styles, culture, the structure of mentoring programs, and the adult learning environment in early care and education settings; and
- Strengthen your ability to articulate your own practice as an early educator, and to adapt your mentoring strategies based on your own skills, your protégé's skills and the context in which you work.

Each chapter concludes with a list of "References and Further Reading." While many of these are cited directly in the text, others are listed as additional resources that provide more information on the major themes of that chapter.

Chapter 1

An Introduction to Mentoring

Few professions are as vital, complex and demanding as the education and care of young children. Whether it takes place in child care centers, family child care homes or other settings, the daily work of early childhood educators makes a profound and lasting difference for children, families and society as a whole. High-quality early care and education (ECE) matters—and research has repeatedly shown that one of the most important ingredients of quality is the presence of well-prepared and well-rewarded teachers.[2]

Yet as demanding as this work is, the expectations placed on early childhood educators[3] are growing. Amid deepening scientific understanding of how critical a child's earliest years are for brain development and lifelong learning,[4] and mounting concern about the academic achievement gap between children of different backgrounds, our profession is increasingly viewed as the key to school readiness and continued success for America's young children. As a result, there is a growing nationwide interest in enhancing quality in early care and education, with many federal, state and local initiatives focused on improving teacher practice.

All of these developments, however, stand in stark contrast with the persistent view among many that early care and education is not a skilled profession. Many early educators continue to have limited access to education and training, with few opportunities for advancement or economic reward.[5] Yet more and more, we are seeing that we cannot guarantee high quality in this field until we guarantee high-quality professional development and support for ECE practitioners.

> ## Mentors and Coaches: A Note on Terminology
>
> While the terms "mentoring" and "coaching" are often used interchangeably, there can be significant distinctions between these two roles. *Mentors* tend to focus on the development of an individual teacher, and goals for the mentoring process are typically agreed upon mutually between the mentor and protégé—although mentoring relationships may differ, depending on the structure and intention of the particular mentoring program. In contrast, *coaches* may work either with individuals or with classroom teams as a group, and/or may have a set agenda for classroom improvement.
>
> Often, however, the distinctions between mentoring and coaching become blurred in practice. We therefore use the terms "mentor" and "mentoring" for the sake of consistency throughout this book, and provide concepts and activities that are relevant for mentors, coaches and others in on-site technical assistance and support roles. We also use the term "protégé" for the person with whom a mentor works; other terms that are sometimes used in the field are "mentee," "peer" or "apprentice."
>
> For further reading on definitions, see Wesley & Buysse (2010) and NAEYC & NACCRRA (2011).

WHAT IS MENTORING?

Mentoring is increasingly seen as a key strategy for supporting teachers at any stage of their careers, and for improving teacher practice. Mentoring is a relationship-based, adult learning strategy intended to promote and support an individual's awareness and refinement of his or her professional learning process and teaching practices.[6] Mentoring pro-

---

2. Whitebook & Ryan, 2011; Kelley & Camilli, 2007; Burchinal, Cryer, Clifford, & Howes, 2002.
3. We use the terms 'teacher' or 'educator' to refer to practitioners in all types of ECE settings—including assistant teachers, head teachers, and family child care providers. We also use feminine pronouns when discussing mentors and protégés, although we recognize that a significant number of men work in this predominantly female profession.
4. National Scientific Council on the Developing Child, 2007.
5. Kagan, Kaurez, & Tarrant, 2008.
6. Wesley & Buysse, 2010.

grams offer teachers a practical and supportive way to learn and grow on the job. They also offer mentors themselves an opportunity to advance in their profession and, often, to earn financial rewards for sharing their skills with others. While mentoring often takes place within the context of a formal program, teachers can form mentoring relationships on their own, perhaps with a trusted director or other colleague. Mentoring, however, is *not* the same as supervision. (See "The Difference Between Mentoring and Supervision," in Chapter 3.)

Mentors are skilled in their craft, creative in problem-solving, keenly observant, able to reflect on their practice, flexible in relating to other adults, ready to learn new information about the process of teaching, and willing to take risks in order to grow.[7] Mentors should have significant experience in teaching young children, with a command of relevant skills and knowledge to share with their protégés about pedagogy and how children learn. Mentoring works best when mentors have received education and training not only in child development, and the care and teaching of young children, but also in adult learning, teacher development and reflective practice.[8] Mentors are open to understanding their protégés

For Mentors Without Extensive ECE Experience

Ideally, mentors have significant experience in teaching young children, with a command of relevant skills and knowledge to share with their protégés about pedagogy and how children learn. In fact, a number of states have established sets of competencies, certification processes and/or training programs for mentors, coaches and other professional development providers in ECE.[9]

If you do not have an extensive background—or if much time has passed since your most recent ECE experience, or if your only teaching experience is with older children—you will need to augment your own preparation in order to strengthen your competencies related to children's learning and early childhood teaching.

Consider the following suggestions:

- Familiarity with your state's *early learning standards* will ground you in what your community considers to be appropriate standards for the learning capabilities of young children of different ages. In addition, your state's *teacher competencies* for early childhood educators will give you a comprehensive picture of the knowledge and skills you will be helping your protégé develop, and will help you assess your own needs for growth and development in order to assist her effectively.

- A course on *early childhood curriculum and teaching* may also be a good place to start. By becoming familiar with the theory and research behind different approaches to teaching young children, you will be better prepared to help your protégé clarify her own assumptions as a teacher, and to offer her alternative strategies to consider.

- If you have not been an ECE teacher yourself, or have not taught recently, other strategies can help build your knowledge. The best option is to spend time in high-quality early learning settings as an observer or volunteer, even for a couple of hours per week. Direct observation or practice will give you a feel for what your protégés face, and if you taught long ago, it can refresh your memory of just how complex an undertaking it is to teach young children well. Perhaps you can visit such programs with your protégé or with other mentors, and talk about the teaching strategies you have observed. You might meet with one or more classroom teachers, and interview them about various teaching approaches you've observed them practicing. See also the listing of resources at the end of the chapter, for other ways to view teachers at work.

As you begin, be sure to find out what mentor competencies, certification processes, or trainings have been established in your community or state.

---

7. Hall, Draper, Smith, & Bullough, 2008.
8. "Reflective practice" has been defined as "the capacity to reflect on action so as to engage in a process of continuous learning" (Schön, 1983).
9. U.S. Department of Health and Human Services, Administration for Children and Families, & Head Start Bureau, 2005; NAEYC & NACCRA, 2011.

from many perspectives—as teachers, as learners, and as members of a community and culture—and they encourage protégés to play an active role in their own learning process.

Mentoring is both *relationship-based* and *content-based*. Mentoring should take place within an open and warm *relationship*, founded in mutual respect for what each person is bringing to the process, but it is more than this: It is a finely tuned balance of support and challenge, focused on encouraging reflection, change and growth.[10] Mentoring also is focused on *content* through the sharing of knowledge: The mentor knows about child development, early learning, and a range of teaching strategies, such as how to support literacy—and as a learner herself, she is also open to researching and finding out about new areas of knowledge along with her protégé. Mentoring can be useful for anyone working with young children, without regard to how long they have been in the field—and protégés can be a very diverse group, with wide variation in education, skills and experience.

✦ ACTIVITY   Questions for Journal Writing

We recommend that you keep a journal of your mentoring experiences to use as a tool for professional growth. Journal entries can be very brief—a passing thought, an anecdote, a question, something your protégé has said—or as lengthy as needed to get a complex idea down on paper. As you begin your work with a protégé, reflect on any or all of the following questions, or write about them in your journal.

1. Has anyone ever been a mentor to you, whether in a formal mentoring program, an ECE setting or another situation? Consider friends, co-workers at current or previous jobs, and others in your community who may have served as role models.
- What did the mentor help you to learn?
- How did your mentor support you in learning?
- What qualities did you appreciate in your mentor?
- What qualities do you think your mentor appreciated about you as a protégé?
- What, if anything, was difficult about the relationship?

2. Have you been a mentor before, whether in an ECE setting or elsewhere?
- Whom did you mentor?
- What did you do to help your protégé to learn?
- In what ways did you feel helpful?
- What qualities do you think your protégé appreciated about you as a mentor?
- What qualities did you appreciate about your protégé?
- In what ways might you like to become more effective as a mentor?

3. Has your own teaching experience focused on the age group of children with whom your protégé(s) work?
- What age level of children do you feel most confident about teaching? Infants and toddlers? Preschoolers? Early elementary? Grades 4 or higher?
- Is your expertise at the age level of the children with whom your protégé works?
- If you have been working with older or younger children than those with whom your protégé works, what strategies will you pursue to build your knowledge and skills?

---

10. Daloz, 1999.

CHANGING LANDSCAPE, ENDURING PRINCIPLES

As a result of increased attention on improving the quality of early care and education, we have seen a steady proliferation of mentoring programs across the country in recent years. This has led to an expansion of the types of settings where mentoring takes place, and of variations in mentoring goals and mentor-protégé relationships. Mentoring historically has been thought of as a strategy to support new teachers, often within the context of their pursuit of higher education, but mentoring now takes place in a wider range of settings, and with protégés whose education and experience vary widely. (For a summary of the variations among mentoring programs, see Table 1.)

Mentoring can take place in a mentor's work setting, perhaps as a component of a protégé's participation in formal training or coursework—or it may take place in a protégé's work setting. Mentoring may be voluntary, or working with a mentor may be a required element of one's job or of a center's participation in a quality improvement initiative. Mentoring may have fairly general and broad goals, or the goals may be narrowly defined or even prescriptive—for example, focused on preparing for an assessment or evaluation, improving a test score, or learning how to use a certain classroom tool or curriculum. Mentoring can also take place over a relatively short period of time, in relation to a specific goal, or it may be a yearlong or multiyear process.

Although mentoring programs vary in structure, the relationship between mentors and protégés has certain basic qualities:

> *The mentor* is an "articulate practitioner,"[11] not only knowledgeable about child learning and development, as well as pedagogical practice with young children, but able to *articulate* this knowledge and skill as she serves as a model and guide to others. She does not supervise the protégé, but rather facilitates learning and development.[12] The mentor provides support to the protégé if she falters, and encourages her when her practice is not all that it could be. The mentor is a trusted counselor who is committed to a close working relationship with the protégé, offering feedback that can move her to a higher level of competence and performance. The mentor has a *disposition* toward learning and growing, too, and is able to appreciate and benefit from the perspectives a protégé can offer.

> *The protégé*, ideally, is equally committed to her own growth and development as a teacher, and to the mentor/protégé relationship. She is willing to learn new skills and reflect upon her practice with children. Like the mentor, she is ready to learn and grow.

? **QUESTIONS FOR DISCUSSION**

Varieties of Mentoring Programs

Table 1 lists how mentoring programs, mentor roles and protégés may differ along several dimensions.

- Which of these variables best apply to your role as a mentor, the program in which you work and the protégés with whom you work?

---

11. Takanishi, 1980.
12. For further discussion, see "The Differences Between Mentoring and Supervision" in Chapter 3.

- How does your role differ from that of others in your mentor training group, or other mentors or coaches you know?
- Practice describing your mentoring program to others, along the dimensions listed in Table 1. What are some of the challenges and opportunities that you may face in your work with protégés as a result of your mentoring program's goals and structure?
- If there are other mentors from your program in your training group, did you all describe your program in the same way? Consider checking with your mentor supervisor about their answers to these questions.

Table 1: Variations in Mentoring Programs

The goals and structures of a mentoring program can have implications for how you are expected to do your job, who your protégés are, and why they are participating. This chart looks at a number of ways in which mentoring programs can differ.

Mentoring programs can vary in **overall purpose**:
- To provide collegial support through informal peer relationships;
- To support the attainment of higher education (e.g., as a student teaching placement) and/or teacher certification;
- To support protégés who are new to the field;
- To improve retention of new and/or experienced teachers;
- To help translate coursework theory into classroom practice;
- To further a quality improvement initiative, such as a Quality Rating and Improvement System or the pursuit of program accreditation; and
- To help implement a curriculum or training model.

The program's **desired outcome**s may be to:
- Achieve higher quality ratings or classroom assessment scores;
- Improve specific instructional practices (such as those focused on early literacy); and
- Improve specific child outcomes (such as language development).

Mentors have varying **work settings** and **job descriptions**. They:
- May work within the same organization as protégés (for example, as a Head Start mentor-coach or within the same school district) or in a different organization;
- May or may not be currently employed as classroom teachers;
- May visit protégés' classrooms, or have protégés visit their classrooms;
- May work with individual protégés or with classroom teams (the latter generally being a "coaching" model);
- May work with one protégé or with multiple protégés at a time;
- May work with protégés who teach a variety of age groups of children within the birth-to-age-8 spectrum;
- May work with protégés within a wide variety of time frames, from a matter of weeks or months to a year or more; and
- May be expected to include directors in various mentoring activities, or may have little involvement with directors.

Individual mentor-protégé **goals and activities** may be:
- Collaboratively developed by the mentor and protégé, or prescribed by the mentoring initiative; and
- Wide-ranging in scope, or focused on particular content areas or skills.

Protégés may have varying **reasons to participate** in mentoring:
- By choice, or as a required part of the job;
- As a component (required or not) of a degree or training program; and
- As a mandate because of classroom quality ratings or other assessments.

Your Mentoring Program

PROGRAM DIMENSIONS	YOUR PROGRAM
What is your mentoring program's overall purpose?	
What are your mentoring program's desired outcomes?	
Where does your mentoring work take place?	
Do you work with protégés individually or in groups? (Include information about number of protégés.)	
How long and how often do you typically work with your protégés?	
Why do protégés participate in the program?	
What is your protégé's role in setting his or her learning goals?	

FOUR MENTORS

Meet Sharon, Lori, Mira and Aisha—a group of mentors with varied professional backgrounds, who work in four different types of program settings. We will return to them in Chapters 3 through 5 as a basis for activities and discussions of various mentoring topics.

Sharon, a mentor teacher employed in a public school system

During her 10 years as a teacher in public preschool and kindergarten classrooms, Sharon discovered how much she enjoyed and learned from talking with other teachers about how they ran their classrooms, made curriculum choices, and worked with children with challenging behaviors. When the local school district advertised for certified teachers to work as mentors in its publicly funded preschool program, Sharon jumped at the opportunity. Assigned to four classrooms serving 3- and 4-year-olds in three different schools, Sharon works with 12 teachers who have varied career histories—newly certified novices, experienced teachers recently assigned to a preschool classroom for the first time, and veteran preschool teachers with decades of experience. (Often, these protégés have paraprofessionals or educational assistants working with them in their classrooms.) Sharon works as a mentor teacher full time, visits each protégé at least twice a month, and is expected to conduct trainings with the protégés as a group, at least twice per semester, on a topic determined by the school district. Sharon participates in an annual two-day mentor training, meets monthly with other mentors and a supervisor to discuss their protégés, and informally discusses her work with other mentors when they are in the district office.

Lori, a mentor teacher whose classroom is an approved
field placement site for early childhood education students

After 25 years of working with preschoolers, Lori's excitement about her work hasn't waned. While she has seen many colleagues over the years leave the classroom for director positions or other leadership roles (and better pay) in the ECE field, Lori has focused on opportunities to serve as a teacher leader, and the Early Childhood Mentor Program in her state provides her with an avenue to do so. Candidates for the coveted role of mentor teacher must undergo a selection process that includes a classroom assessment, an in-person interview, and a reference check. Once selected, mentors participate in an ongoing monthly seminar designed to prepare teachers for their mentoring roles. The seminar also serves as a learning community in which mentors can share issues that arise in working with their protégés. Early childhood education students attending the local community college visit mentors' classrooms to decide where they would like to be assigned for their semester-long, two-half-days-per-week field placement. Lori is a popular mentor, typically working with two or three protégés each semester. These may be younger students who have not yet worked as teachers, or more experienced students employed as early childhood teachers (some of them for many years) who are now pursuing a college degree, perhaps in response to new requirements. Lori and other mentors receive stipends each semester for their work; the amount is based on the number of students assigned to their classrooms.

Mira, a coach who works with a Quality Rating and Improvement System (QRIS)

Mira became a coach with her state's ECE Quality Rating and Improvement System (QRIS) when the local child care resource and referral agency, where she worked providing referrals to parents, was awarded a QRIS technical assistance contract. Candidates for mentor positions were required to have a bachelor's degree and some work experience with young children. Mira had worked part time in a child care center several years earlier, while earning her degree in social work. Mira works with 10 family child care providers who have chosen to participate in the QRIS, and with 10 classroom teams of teachers and teaching assistants (in five centers) whose directors have chosen to participate in the QRIS. Her protégés' ECE experience and education levels vary widely. In preparation for their coaching roles, Mira and her colleagues have participated in a weeklong training on how to use the Environment Rating Scales[13] in participating child care homes and centers, and attend biweekly meetings for coaches.

Aisha, a mentor who assists teachers with implementing
a specific preschool science curriculum

A recent college graduate with a degree in psychology, Aisha knew she wanted to work with people, but wasn't sure what form this would take. An advertisement for a one-year position, as a mentor to help preschool teachers implement a certain curriculum model, caught her eye. She met the qualifications: a four-year degree, with some prior work experience with young children. Aisha and her fellow mentors participated in a two-week training focused on the particular curriculum model they would be using. About half of the 20 mentors in the group were former preschool teachers; the others, like Aisha, had some experience working with young children, but not in an ECE setting. Each mentor in her program is assigned to work with 20 sites over a 10-week period, visiting two child care classrooms or homes per day for 10 weeks. In addition to the classroom visits, Aisha provides training for groups of teachers within the center who are learning the curriculum model together.

---

13. Harms, Clifford, & Cryer, 1998; Harms, Cryer, & Clifford, 2003; Harms, Cryer, & Clifford, 2007.

Which of the four mentors profiled here—Sharon, Lori, Mira and Aisha—works in a mentoring program most like yours? Consider the following dimensions:

- Purpose and desired outcomes of the mentoring program/initiative;
- Mentor's and protégés' work settings;
- Mentor's job expectations (e.g., number of protégés, frequency of contact with protégé, etc.); and
- Terms of protégé participation.

HOW THIS BOOK IS ORGANIZED: ASSUMPTIONS AND PRINCIPLES

This book proceeds from the general assumption that mentors already have a significant background in child learning and development, as well as teaching experience with young children—although we recognize that sometimes this is not the case. (See "For Mentors Without Extensive ECE Experience," above.) The book therefore aims to build upon such knowledge and experience by addressing the additional knowledge and skill areas that are fundamental to mentoring. Chapter 2 explores theories of adult learning, Chapter 3 explores the varied individual, social and environmental factors that influence adult learning, and Chapters 4 and 5 focus on building specific mentoring skills and competencies.

Further, drawing from the experience of the many early childhood mentoring programs that have developed throughout the United States, this book shares a core set of assumptions and principles about the mentoring process:

- The growth and development of children, and of adults, in early childhood settings are vitally linked.
- Like children, most adults learn best by having practical, job-related, hands-on opportunities to apply new ideas and information to real-life situations.[14] The mentoring process provides a context for practicing and applying new skills, and for receiving guidance in teaching and caregiving practice.
- The first years of teaching are an especially important time for learning and growing,[15] but effective mentoring can take place at *any* stage of an educator's career.
- Mentors should be directly experienced in the area(s) in which they are mentoring or coaching others.
- To be most effective, a mentor should be trained as one. While a mentor should have considerable experience and skill in early care and education, including child development and pedagogy, she also should receive training and support in the areas of adult learning and teacher development.
- Mentoring is not the same as supervision.
- A mentor is also a learner, and needs support both as a teacher and as a learner.

Mentoring can help an early care and education program to become a better "community of learners"—a place where both children and adults are encouraged to reach their full potential. While mentoring is only one response to the professional preparation and

---

14. Merriam & Caffarella, 1999.
15. National Scientific Council on the Developing Child, 2007.

growth of early childhood educators, it has great potential for transforming the nature of early care and education practice. If you are interested in working with other educators to help them engage in learning and reflection to improve their practice, this book is for you. The following chapter is devoted to understanding how adults learn and change.

 **Activity**   The Skills That I Bring to a Mentoring Relationship

Thinking about yourself as you embark on or continue your development as a mentor, assess your strengths below.

I CONSIDER MYSELF:	VERY DEVELOPED 1	SOMEWHAT DEVELOPED 2	NOT YET DEVELOPED 3
Skilled as a teacher of young children			
Keenly observant of children and teachers			
Skilled at teaching children from diverse cultural, ethnic, and economic backgrounds			
Creative in problem solving			
Willing to evaluate and change my practice			
Able to understand other teachers' points of view			
Able to adapt my approach to different teachers			
Open to learning new information about the teaching process			
Willing to take risks in order to grow			
Supportive of others as they learn and grow			
Open to feedback from others			
Educated about how children learn and how to teach them			
Educated about adult learning and teacher development			
Skilled in explaining my teaching practices and how they promote children's learning			

Based on your answers above:
• What are the three greatest strengths that you bring to the mentoring role?
• Name three areas in which you would like to learn more in order to be a successful mentor.

Your answers to these questions will help you identify your own personal learning goals as a mentor. Repeating the survey periodically will help you to measure progress toward your own learning goals.

REFERENCES AND FURTHER READING

Burchinal, M. R., Cryer, D., Clifford, R. M. & Howes, C. (2002). Caregiver training and classroom quality in child care centers. *Applied Developmental Science, 6*(1), 2-11.

Buysse, V. & Wesley, P. (2005). *Consultation in early childhood settings.* Baltimore: Brookes Publishing Co.

Crane, T. (2010). *The heart of coaching: How to use transformational coaching to create a high-performance coaching culture.* San Diego, CA: FTA Press.

Daloz, L. A. (1999). *Mentor: Guiding the journey of adult learners.* San Francisco: Jossey-Bass.

Garavuso, V. (2009). *Being mentored: Getting what you need.* New York: McGraw-Hill, Practical Guide Series.

Hall, K. M., Draper, R. J., Smith, L. K. & Bullough, R. V. (2008). More than a place to teach: Exploring the perceptions of the roles and responsibilities of mentor teachers. *Mentoring and Tutoring: Partnership in Learning, 16*(3), 328-345.

Harms, T., Clifford, R. &, Cryer, D. (1998). *The Early Childhood Environment Rating Scale-Revised.* New York, NY: Teachers College Press.

Harms, T., Cryer, D. & Clifford, R. (2007). *Family Child Care Environment Rating Scale, Revised Edition.* New York, NY: Teachers College Press.

Harms, T., Cryer, D., Clifford, R. (2003). *Infant Toddler Environment Rating Scale, Revised Edition.* New York, NY: Teachers College Press.

Kagan, S.L., Kaurez, K. & Tarrant, K. (2008). *The early care and education teaching workforce at the fulcrum: An agenda for reform.* New York: Teachers College Press.

Kelley, P., & Camilli, G. (2007). *The impact of teacher education on outcomes in center-based early childhood education programs: A meta-analysis.* New Brunswick, NJ: National Institute for Early Education Research.

Merriam, S. B., & Caffarella, R. S. (1999). *Learning in adulthood: A comprehensive guide.* (2nd edition). San Francisco, CA: Jossey-Bass.

National Association for the Education of Young Children (NAEYC) and National Association of Child Care Resource & Referral Agencies (NACCRRA) (2011). Early childhood education professional development: Training and technical assistance glossary. Washington, DC: NAEYC & NACCRRA.

National Scientific Council on the Developing Child (2007). The science of early childhood development. http://www.developingchild.net.

Nolan, M. (2006). *Mentor coaching and leadership in early care and education.* Belmont, CA: Wadsworth Publishing.

Rush, D. & Sheldon, M. (2011). *The early childhood coaching handbook.* Baltimore: Brookes Publishing Co.

Schön, D. (1983). *The reflective practitioner: How professionals think in action.* New York: Basic Books.

Smith, S., Schneider, W. & Kreader, J. L. (2010). Features of professional development and on-site assistance in child care quality rating improvement systems: A survey of state-wide systems. *National Center for Children in Poverty.* Retrieved from: http://www.nccp.org/.

Takanishi, R. (1980). The unknown teacher: Symbolic and structural issues in teacher education. Keynote speech presented at the Midwest AEYC Conference, Milwaukee, WI, 1980.

U.S. Department of Health and Human Services, Administration for Children and Families, and Head Start Bureau (2005). Mentor-Coach Manual. Washington, D.C.: Head Start Bureau.

Wesley, P. W. & Buysse, V. (2010). *The quest for quality: Promising innovations for early childhood programs*. Baltimore: Brooks Publishing Co.

Whitebook, M. & Ryan, S. (2011). Degrees in context: Asking the right questions about preparing skilled and effective teachers of young children. *Preschool Policy Brief (22)*. New Brunswick, NJ: National Institute for Early Education Research.

Zachary, L. & Fischler, L. (2009). *The mentor's guide: Facilitating effective learning relationships*. San Francisco: Jossey-Bass.

Chapter 2

Understanding Adult Learning

The mentoring experience, for both mentors and protégés, is about learning. Therefore, reflecting on your own learning experiences as an adult—whether in a classroom with young children, or related to something outside your work life—can be a good starting place for understanding adult learning and for building your mentoring skills.

Most of us can easily recall situations in which we were able to solve a problem or meet a challenge—and the processes by which we did so lie at the heart of learning. We can probably recall instances, too, of being stuck in misunderstanding or confusion, unable to move forward. The difference between success and frustration can tell us a lot about how we and other adults learn. Keeping your own learning experiences in mind can help you understand and evaluate what experts say about adult learning—and these experiences can be the foundation for understanding other adults whose learning you will want to facilitate through mentoring.

THEORIES OF ADULT LEARNING

Most contemporary adult learning theories draw on *constructivist*[16] frameworks—the same theories that are typically studied in child development and teacher education courses. Whether applied to children or to adults, constructivist theory defines problem-solving as the center of learning, thinking and development. When children solve problems and understand the consequences of their actions—for example, placing a block in front of a ball to keep it from rolling down the slide—they can *construct* or build on what they have learned by applying it to other situations and experimenting with their environments. In this instance, the child might come to understand, "I could put something in front of other things that roll."

So it is with adults. While adults can read to acquire new information or skills, or listen for more extended periods than young children can, they also learn, as children do, through active participation in real-life activities.[17] As a result, to take one example, simply reading about early childhood development (vital as it may be) is insufficient for learning to be a teacher. Hands-on experiences, such as student teaching, are increasingly seen as fundamental to teacher preparation and ongoing professional development.[18] It's not enough to be told what to do, or to read about it; we need to apply what we are learning, and build on past experience, through practice.

The constructivist theory of learning holds that children and adults continually build on past experiences to form new theories and test hypotheses, and that this process is what leads to "constructing" knowledge and solving problems. We don't learn when people tell us what to know, but when we are engaged in thinking about, and thinking through, our problems and challenges. Consider another example. Adults who were well into adulthood before using a computer or a cellphone may experience much more difficulty in understanding touch screens, new software or other technological change than someone who has grown up with digital devices and takes them for granted. Even when faced with new equipment or software applications, younger people may find it relatively easier to figure out

---

16. Dewey, 1938, 1997.
17. Rogoff, 1990.
18. Darling-Hammond & Hammerness, 2005; Darling-Hammond, 2006; National Center for Accreditation of Teacher Education, 2010.

and adapt to such a situation, because prior experience has armed them with strategies for approaching similar problems.

Two constructivist theorists commonly studied in the field of child development—*Jean Piaget* (1896-1980) and *Lev Vygotsky* (1896-1934)—provide useful concepts for understanding adult learning.

According to Piaget's theory, learners are motivated by a need for *equilibrium*: We want what we know to be in balance with what we experience.[19] Consider the teacher who finds that the cleanup routines that worked with 4-year-olds in last year's class are ineffective this year. Where a five-minute warning used to work well in helping children finish what they were doing and make transitions, this year it's practically a signal to take out more activities and get even busier before time runs out. Drawing on prior knowledge (that this strategy has worked before) and applying it to the new group (what Piaget calls "assimilation"), the teacher experiences disequilibrium when the five-minute warning is unsuccessful. So she tries a new strategy (what Piaget calls a process of "adaptation" and "accommodation") to solve the cleanup problem and achieve a new equilibrium. Starting about 10 minutes before the transition time, she now makes her way around the room at least once, quietly asking each child to begin getting ready to put things away. The teacher has found that a general five-minute announcement doesn't work in every situation, and so she draws on prior knowledge (that warnings are important) and experiments with a more individualized approach. In adapting her knowledge by accommodating new information, she has *constructed* a more sophisticated understanding of managing children's transitions.

Vygotsky, using a different lens, viewed learning as a result not only of individual processes but of *social* processes—primarily, interactions with more knowledgeable others during real-life activities.[20] For children, these "others" may be adults or older children, and in the professional world of early care and education, they could be mentors, directors, fellow teachers, or teacher educators. The knowledgeable other understands both what the learner can do on her own, and what she could master next, first with assistance, and then independently. Vygotsky called this area of gradual learning the *zone of proximal development*.

Consider "circle time" in a preschool classroom. Perhaps a protégé is skilled at working with small groups of children, but has never led a circle time with the entire class, which is her goal. The protégé might observe the mentor leading the circle, later discussing the strategies the mentor used and how they worked. Next, the protégé might try some of these strategies when reading with a smaller group of children. After that, the mentor and protégé might co-lead a circle time, or the mentor might play a leading role for only part of it. Following this, the protégé could lead the circle on her own, with the mentor present to observe or help, before eventually doing this activity independently. Over time, the mentor might occasionally observe the protégé and give feedback—or might even ask the protégé to give *her* feedback on a circle time or related activity, to demonstrate how even a "knowledgeable other" is always working to strengthen her skills. The mentor's goal is to help the protégé move through this particular "zone of proximal development"—from awareness of the skill to practicing it, and finally, to using it flexibly and independently.

Piaget and Vygotsky, along with John Dewey and others, developed constructivist theories of learning in the first half of the 20th century. Drawing on their work, later theorists have articulated particular conceptions of *adult* learning. In formulating a field of study

---

19. Piaget, 1985.
20. Vygotsky, 1978.

called *andragogy*—learning strategies focused on adults—*Malcolm Knowles* (1913-1997) identified three key principles:[21]

Self-direction. Adults have their own motivations for learning, and even when they depend on others, they seek autonomy and independence. This means that adults learn best when they are seeking to learn (not merely being told to do so), and when the subject matter fits their own purposes.

Need for knowledge. Adult learners are motivated by real-life problems they are facing, and therefore tend to be most interested in types of learning that have immediate application. As a result, ECE teachers may generally be most drawn to classes or other professional development opportunities that seem most relevant to the challenges and goals of their classrooms.

Experience. Adults build on what they know and have experienced, so it is critical to engage adult learners by building on their current understanding and providing relevant new experiences. As a mentor, you may find that protégés who are able to participate in setting their learning goals will view the mentoring relationship as more relevant to their experience. In addition, taking the time to assess protégés' knowledge and skills can help mentors target learning experiences to the protégé's zone of proximal development, so that these are neither too basic nor too advanced. Similarly, for you, your mentor training will be most meaningful if it acknowledges and builds on the prior experiences that have readied you for this new role.

 **Journal Activity**

Questions for Journal Writing

1. Think about a learning experience that you felt was successful. Why did you consider it a success? Did you feel confident about your learning process throughout the experience, or only in retrospect? (For example, did you feel any of what Piaget might call "disequilibrium" as you learned a new task or body of information?)

2. What role have "knowledgeable others" (to use Vygotsky's term) played in supporting—or even undermining—your learning? Describe a situation in which another person has been a helpful guide, and perhaps another in which someone has made learning more difficult.

ADULT LEARNING STYLES

From observing children—whether in a classroom or park, or in your family—you know that they do not all approach problem-solving, and learning, in the same way. Some, for example, tend to sit back and watch at first, while others are more immediately active. Some babies wait to take their first steps until they can stand unassisted without falling, while others eagerly try walking as soon as they can pull themselves up. As teachers, we often use information about how individual children approach learning, in order to structure activities that will enable them to feel challenged yet successful. Adults, too, have varied learning styles.

David A. Kolb was among the first theorists to consider the variety of adult approaches to learning—the different ways in which we process new experiences and information.[22] Kolb formulated a four-stage cycle to describe these varied learning approaches, based on individuals' own styles. He holds that immediate experiences provide the basis for observation, reflection, thinking and action. When a problem arises, for example, a person decides, based on his or her learning style, whether to jump in to learn how to tackle the problem, or to hold

---

21. Knowles, 1975, 1990.
22. Kolb, 1984.

back a bit and continue observing in order to learn more. At the same time, each person processes information, and makes sense of it, primarily by thinking or by feeling.

In other words, Kolb classifies how learners tend to approach a task as either (1) active experimentation (doing) or (2) reflective observation (watching), and then how they transform the experience into something meaningful as either (3) abstract conceptualization (thinking, analyzing, planning) or (4) concrete experience (feeling). In Kolb's schema, how a learner approaches a task (doing or watching) and how that learner makes meaning of it (thinking or feeling) together constitute the person's learning style. The following are brief descriptions of these styles.

> *Watching and feeling.* These learners frequently rely on brainstorming and generating ideas to solve problems. They are also able to see other people's points of view, and frequently want information on alternative views of a situation or idea. They enjoy working in groups and are skilled at interpersonal communication.

> *Watching and thinking.* These learners use inductive reasoning to solve problems and to make theoretical models. They prefer clear, concise, logical explanations, and frequently rely on reading to gather information for solving problems, as opposed to gaining knowledge through practical experience.

> *Doing and feeling.* These learners rely on intuition rather than logic, often rely on other people's ideas, and enjoy a hands-on approach to solving problems. They are attracted to new ideas, and can flexibly change and accommodate new information.

Adult Learning Styles in ECE: One Example

To take an example from early care and education, consider how a variety of protégés with different learning styles might approach the subject of dual-language learning among young children. While these teachers all are interested in making their classrooms more supportive and enriching for children whose home language is not English, the teachers all will not learn most effectively in the same way.

"Watching and feeling" learners: These adults might learn best by observing other teachers on video or in person, followed by a small group discussion. For instance, the protégé could observe how another teacher employs a variety of nonverbal cues (such as pictures and gestures), as well as vocabulary in more than one language, to help children master English while building on their home languages. The observation could then be a starting point for discussing with co-teachers or the mentor how such strategies could be incorporated into the protégé's classroom practice.

"Watching and thinking" learners: Observation is also important for these learners, but they may be more inclined to do some further reading about dual-language strategies before engaging in discussion, perhaps even writing a plan for how they might use various strategies in the classroom.

"Doing and feeling" learners: While observing others is useful for all learners, these adults might benefit more, as an entry point, from being observed in the classroom themselves, and then receiving feedback about other approaches to try with children in a multilingual classroom.

"Doing and thinking" learners: For these learners, it might work well to try an activity and analyze how it could be improved, read or hear information about dual-language strategies, and then craft a change in approach. Take a teacher who leads her group in a neighborhood walk to gather fall leaves and other items of interest. When she notices that the three Hmong-speaking children do not gather anything in their bags without prompting from an adult, and then show no interest in talking about or sharing their finds with others, she realizes, in discussion with her mentor, that she might have been better prepared for the trip by speaking to all the parents in advance; learning about any "home rules" for picking up objects from the street or the ground; and including vocabulary words in multiple languages, including Hmong, when introducing the activity to the children.

Doing and thinking. These learners use deductive reasoning to solve problems and to focus on a specific problem at hand. They tend not to prefer interpersonal communication.

Kolb also holds that as adults develop, they become increasingly able to use different learning styles, but that at the beginning of one's career, when many concepts are new, learners tend to stick with their preferred style.

Learning theorist *Barbara Rogoff* has focused on "cultural ways of learning"—the ways in which taking in new information, and approaching a problem or task, can be strongly influenced by our families and cultures of origin.[23] Culture, in fact, is often described as not only a set of values and beliefs, but also as the configuration of ways in which people perceive information and make meaning of their worlds. Culture influences the types of learning experiences that a given society values, and in which children participate. These experiences can develop into specific cultural learning styles and shape how children and eventually adults approach learning. Some cultures, for example, may place a higher value on independent learning and individual achievement, while others may favor cooperative learning and being part of a community. Some may emphasize learning through the spoken word, others the written word.

As a mentor, it will be important for you to gain an understanding of your protégé's learning style, as well as your own. This can help you understand how she might approach a task (and how this may differ from how you would approach it), and can help you structure the types of activities that are most meaningful to your protégé as a learner. Keep in mind, too, that "learning style" is not necessarily something a protégé will readily be able to articulate about herself. One of your mentoring roles might be to help her better describe herself as a learner—for example, by exploring recent or past learning experiences with her.

Activity | Learning Styles

Learning is an enriching part of our lives, but we do not all approach learning in the same way. Understanding ourselves and others as learners can help you as a mentor in building a toolbox of skills that support different learning styles.

Consider the example of how people might approach learning a new game For this activity, you and your fellow mentors will learn the game of Royal Parade, a form of Solitaire. (Or, if you prefer, select a new game that teachers might use with young children.) You may go about learning it in any way that feels comfortable to you: You can ask someone to show you, read about it in a book or on a website, watch someone else play the game first, or just jump right in.

Questions for Discussion:
- What were the steps you took to learn Royal Parade?
- Did you encounter any challenges along the way; if so, how did you resolve them?
- Did mistakes play any role in your learning?
- How did your approach differ from others in your group?
- Did people who had never played any type of Solitaire before approach the challenge differently than those who had at least some knowledge of Solitaire?

STAGE THEORIES OF ADULT DEVELOPMENT

Theorists have also thought about adult learning in terms of development over time. *Stage theorists* suggest that there is a succession of major life tasks to be completed by each person as he or she grows. These tasks are usually accompanied by conflicts that have to be resolved at certain points in our lives. Stages of development are fluid, of course, with not all adults meeting the same changes and challenges at the same time of their lives.

Erik Erikson (1902-1994), for example, held that *young adulthood* is a time when the primary conflict is between making close friends with others and being "on one's own,"

---

23. Rogoff, 1990.

becoming independent. Erikson's theory also includes the *maturity* phase (midlife), when the conflict we may face is between focusing on our own accomplishments, and sharing our knowledge or expertise with others, often younger people (a process he called "generativity"). The choice to become a mentor for other teachers is a significant example of such a midlife maturity phase. Erikson considered the dominant conflict in *old age* (later life) to be between integrity or pride in one's life achievements, and the challenge of getting older and losing one's physical abilities. Each of these major phases, according to the theory, may last for years. They chart a course in which successful resolution of conflict results in a new capacity to interact with what life has to offer.[24]

Since, broadly speaking, different issues in need of resolution commonly rise to the surface for us at various times at our lives, we may find that our age peers are experiencing similar challenges or conflicts. Being aware of what development issues are "up" for you, what may be up for your protégé, and whether your protégé is in a stage you have experienced or not, can be helpful in thinking about the relationship.

Another way to think about stages of adult development is through the change and growth that adults experience in how they make meaning—also known as their "ways of knowing." An adult's underlying meaning system provides a filter through which she views the world, and shapes her interpretations and behaviors. Adults, like children, move gradually from simpler to more complex ways of knowing. With adults, moving from one sequential developmental stage to another is not necessarily a matter of age. Adults grow and change at their own pace, based on the support available to them and the challenges they face.

Robert Kegan has posited three stages of "adult knowing."[25] The first is *instrumental*. In this stage, adults view knowledge as a set of rules to be followed that are right or wrong. Within the early childhood classroom, teachers in the instrumental stage might view disciplinary techniques as valid if, for instance, they result in children doing what they are told, without yet thinking about the underlying causes of children's behaviors. When these teachers participate in mentoring relationships, they may rely on the mentor to tell them what to do and how to learn, and may view mentoring, for example, as a way to increase compliance with standards rather than as a more nuanced process of teaching and learning.

In the second stage, *socializing*, adults view knowledge in relationship to others, and see it as coming from a higher authority. In early childhood classrooms, teachers may base their values about how to teach on experts in the field, for instance, not yet taking into full consideration the individual needs of the children they are teaching. Within the mentoring relationship, protégés in the socializing stage may expect mentors to tell them what to do and learn, in order to be able to fulfill their teaching roles properly.

Finally, adults in the *self-authoring* stage view themselves and their experiences as one important source of knowledge among many. In this respect, knowledge about teaching and learning, for example, is generated through one's own interpretations and evaluations of values, standards, perceptions, predictions and context. A teacher in the self-authoring stage may then be able to adjust her teaching flexibly when she notices that a particular activity is not engaging some of the children, rather than simply continuing to follow the prescribed curriculum or the mentor's advice. Within mentoring relationships, protégés in the self-authoring stage may expect mentors to help them meet their own articulated goals.

---

24. Erikson, 1950.
25. Kegan, 1994.

Certain stage theorists have postulated stages of *teacher development* that complement Kegan's stages of adult ways of knowing. As Malcolm Knowles noted, adults learn best when what they are learning is important to them and addresses immediate needs. Understanding phases of teacher development, and what teachers are likely to be concerned with during different phases of their careers, can help you and your protégé pinpoint relevant areas for learning and growth—and may also help explain why you and your protégé, at various times, might weigh such priority areas differently.

David Berliner has developed five stages of teacher development.[26] In his first stage, the *novice teacher* tends to adhere to rules strictly, making instructional decisions with little regard to context, and is therefore often unable to predict children's behaviors and responses. As she moves into the *advanced beginner* stage, she begins to develop strategic knowledge about teaching, and improves her practice in the timing and delivery of instruction. In the *competency* stage, she is able to set goals for learning and to focus increasingly on whether, how and what children are learning. As she moves into the stages of *proficiency* and *expertise*, she is able to apply instructional techniques flexibly, based on the individual needs of children, and takes classroom context into consideration in all her decision-making.

In mentoring situations, protégés at different stages require different types of supports and learning opportunities. The novice and advanced beginner may need support in building a vocabulary for teaching and learning, and for building reflection skills, in order to begin evaluating the success of their instruction and the unique needs of children. Advanced beginners and competent teachers may need support in connecting theory to practice, and in developing an expanded repertoire of instructional techniques, often through mentor modeling. Finally, proficient and expert teachers may need help in developing their skills at articulating what they do and how they make teaching decisions, in order to prepare to mentor new teachers themselves.

Early childhood education professor *Lilian Katz* has developed a four-stage framework for thinking specifically about *preschool teacher development*, and the types of professional development that may be most relevant to them during each stage.[27] (Note that the length of time a teacher spends in each stage can vary greatly, and teachers may revisit a stage, for example, if they find themselves working with an age group of children that is new to them.) Katz's work posits that although new and experienced ECE teachers are at different stages of growth, they are all traveling along the same basic path:

- *Survival stage*: Mainly concerned with surviving, the teacher realizes the discrepancy between anticipated success and classroom realities; might feel inadequate and unprepared.
- *Consolidation stage* (second and third years of teaching): Consolidates gains made in the first stage; teacher begins to focus on individual children and differentiates specific skills and tasks to be mastered next.
- *Renewal stage* (third and fourth years of teaching): Might tire of doing the same things, and want to look for innovations in the field.
- *Maturity stage* (three or more years of teaching): Has come to terms with herself as a teacher; asks deeper and more abstract questions.

---

26. Berliner, 1998.
27. Katz, 1972.

1. Stages of Teacher Development

Teachers are all at different stages of development. Some are new to the field; others may have a few years of experience, and are beginning to feel comfortable in their teaching role; and others have years of experience under their belts. Their stages of development can have implications for the challenges they face and the kinds of support they need. In this activity, you will interview three teachers at three different stages of development (novice, moderately experienced and "seasoned"), asking each teacher the following:

- Describe a challenge related to teaching that you have experienced in the past year.
- Describe a success or improvement related to teaching that you have experienced in the past year.
- Describe your current teaching goals. What are a couple of things that you are working on, or hoping to improve in your teaching practice, in the coming year?

Questions for Discussion:
- Compare teachers *within* each stage of development. What are the commonalities, and what are the differences?
- Compare teachers *across* stages of development. What are the commonalities, and what are the differences?

- What are the implications of a protégé's stage of development for your work as a mentor?

2. Stages of Adult Development

Over the course of our adult lives, our interests, challenges and pleasures often change. For this activity, each person in the mentor group should write down three words or phrases that describe her current chronological age and stage of life (for example, "starting a new career," "busier than ever," "slowing down," "preoccupied with my adult children," "caring for elders"). On the other side of the paper, each should write down her current decade of life (20s, 30s, 40s, etc.). Display the descriptions, according to decade, on a table or wall where everyone can view them.

Questions for Discussion:
- What differences and similarities did you notice among the decades?
- What surprised you about others' descriptions of the decade you are in?
- What surprised you about others' descriptions of decades you have already or have not yet experienced?
- What are you learning about yourself during this decade of your life?

Although there is some disagreement about the number of stages involved in teacher development, all researchers agree that the level of complexity of learning and development increases as teachers grow in their work: from concern with self and survival, to a more child-centered orientation; from insecurity, to confidence in one's performance; from the use of a small variety of teaching and caregiving strategies, to an ever expanding collection of strategies to meet the needs of the diverse children in one's care; from a fear of change, to an acceptance that change is an essential process of life; and from concern with their own classrooms, to a wider commitment to the ECE profession and a greater involvement in professional activities.

* * * * * *

This chapter has presented various theories about adults as learners. Some theorists propose explanations about the process of learning, others about the phases of learning, and others about variations in how adults approach learning or become most receptive to it. Some of these proposed explanations may resonate for you more than others, but each can be seen as a tool to help you understand your own learning or that of your protégé.

REFERENCES AND FURTHER READING

Bergen, S. (2009). *Best practices for training early childhood professionals.* St. Paul, MN: Redleaf Press.

Berliner, D. (1988). *The development of expertise in pedagogy.* Paper presented at the meeting of the American Association of Colleges for Teacher Education, New Orleans, LA, February 1988.

Darling-Hammond, L. (2006). *Powerful teacher education: Lessons from exemplary programs.* San Francisco, CA: Jossey-Bass.

Darling-Hammond, L. & Hammerness, K., with Grossman, P., Rust, F. & Shulman, L. (2005). The design of teacher education programs, in *Preparing teachers for a changing world: What teachers should learn and be able to do.* San Francisco, CA: Jossey-Bass.

Dewey, J. (1938, 1997). Experience and education. New York: Macmillan.

Erikson, E.H. (1950). *Childhood and Society.* New York: Norton.

Garavuso, V. (2009). *Being mentored: Getting what you need.* New York: McGraw-Hill, Practical Guide Series.

Gardner, H. (2011). *Frames of mind: The theory of multiple intelligences.* New York: Basic Books. Tenth anniversary edition, with new introduction. New York: Basic Books.

Gilligan, C. (1982). *In a different voice.* Cambridge, MA: Harvard University Press.

Irvine, J.J. & York, D.E. (1995). Learning styles and culturally diverse students: A literature review. In J.A. Banks (Ed.), *Handbook of Research on Multicultural Education*, 484-97. New York: Simon & Schuster-Macmillan.

Katz, L. (1972). The developmental stages of preschool teachers. *Elementary School Journal*, 73(1), 50-54.

Kegan, R. (1994). *In over our heads: The mental demands of modern life.* Cambridge, MA: Harvard University Press.

Knowles, M.S. (1975). *Self-directed learning: A guide for learners and teachers.* Englewood Cliffs, NJ: Prentice Hall/Cambridge.

Knowles, M. S. (1990). *The adult learner: A neglected species.* Revised Edition. Houston: Gulf Publishing Company.

Kolb, D.A. (1984). *Experiential learning.* Englewood Cliffs, NJ: Prentice-Hall.

Merriam, S., Caffarella, M., & Baumgartner, L. (2012). *Learning in adulthood: A comprehensive guide*, third edition. San Francisco, CA: Jossey-Bass.

National Council for Accreditation of Teacher Education (2010). *Transforming teacher education through clinical practice: A national strategy to prepare effective teachers.* Washington, DC: National Council for Accreditation of Teacher Education.

Piaget, J. (1985). *Equilibration of cognitive structures.* Chicago: University of Chicago Press.

Rogoff, B. (1990). *Apprenticeship in thinking: Cognitive development in social context.* New York: Oxford University Press.

Ross-Gordon, J.M. (2003). Adult learners in the classroom. Wiley Periodicals, Inc.: New Directions for Student Services, No. 102, Summer 2003.

Taylor, K., Marienau, C. & Fiddler, M. (2000). Women's ways of knowing. In *Developing adult learners: Strategies for teachers and trainers*. San Francisco: Jossey-Bass.

Vygotsky, L. S. (1978). *Mind in society: The development of higher psychological processes.* Cambridge, MA: Harvard University Press.

Chapter 3

Building a Relationship with Your Protégé

GETTING STARTED

The start of any mentor/protégé relationship, whether it is your first or one of many you've experienced, involves two-way exploration. You will want to discover what your protégé hopes to gain from working with you, and she, in turn, will want to know about your early childhood teaching experience and how and why you came to be a mentor. Thinking about your initial interactions with your protégé is one of your first tasks in establishing a productive learning relationship. The "getting to know you" dance involves four basic steps:

Step One: Person to Person

When first meeting your protégé, rely on tools you use when you meet or chat with people at a party, class or other event. Brief, casual chat acknowledges that the role of mentor or protégé is only one of many in your life, and signals your understanding of your protégé as a whole person with a range of experiences—different from your own—that she brings to her work.

Step Two: Teacher to Teacher

While it is tempting to begin your foray into early childhood topics by discussing the goals and expectations of the mentor-protégé relationship, moving too soon to this conversation may constrict the collaborative relationship you are trying to establish and the personal connection necessary for it to thrive. Sharing some details with each other about your journeys in the field—how long you have been teaching, the ages of children you've worked with, the types of programs and job roles you have experienced—will provide you and your protégé with important information. Next, ask your protégé what she considers to be going well in her classroom. Such a question signals that you recognize her as a teacher who brings her own expertise to the mentor-protégé relationship.

Sharing information about your own experience as a teacher—activities you find easy or difficult to implement with children, teaching skills about which you feel more or less confident, examples of how your teaching practice has improved over time—shows, by example, that you understand it's an ongoing process to develop one's expertise as a teacher. It frames your relationship as one between two professionals in different stages of their development, rather than between a "superior" and "inferior" practitioner. This is particularly important if your protégé is more skilled or experienced than you in certain aspects of teaching.

Step Three: Learner to Learner

Invite your protégé to tell you about something she has learned in the last year, such as a skill or a body of information; it doesn't have to be about teaching young children. Ask how she went about learning: Did she seek help from another person, watch someone demonstrate, read about it online or at the library? What did she like about or find lacking in this approach? Share, too, some new skill or knowledge you have acquired. A conversation about a successful learning experience, unrelated to your roles as mentor or protégé, can be a comfortable way to begin your joint exploration of the learning process, and with sensitive listening and questioning, it can teach you about how your protégé approaches learning.

You can also use the conversation to introduce the concept of learning styles, and sharing your experiences as a learner may open your protégé to considering different approaches to her own learning.

Step Four: Protégé to Mentor

Following up on that discussion, ask your protégé how she likes to go about learning for work, whether through reading, observing, watching demonstrations, or in other ways. This doesn't mean you will be restricted to using the modality she prefers, but it can guide you toward how to begin working together, and may put your protégé more at ease. After these first steps, ask your protégé about skills she would like to build, and things she might want to try for the first time, or approach differently, in her classroom.

Discussing what your protégé would like to explore will allow you to assess how closely her learning aspirations align with the stated goals of your mentoring program; don't be surprised if they seem too narrow, too broad, or unrelated. Part of your work as a mentor, and one of the skills you will build over time, is to incorporate into the mentoring experience what your protégé considers relevant and important. Sometimes this requires only a minor adjustment, but at other times, rethinking or reframing may be necessary to build a bridge between the expectations of the mentoring program and what your protégé wants to work on—an issue we discuss later in this chapter.

 **Activity** | **"Getting to Know You" as a Group**

Mira and Aisha work with groups of protégés, while Lori and Sharon work with individuals. How might Mira and Aisha approach the "getting to know you" dance differently from Lori and Sharon?

Person to person: For an icebreaker, Mira often asks protégés to pair off and "interview" each other about something they like to do outside of work. Then she asks them to share with the group what they learned about the other person. She finds that this works best when protégés don't already know each other well. What might she use as an icebreaker when the protégés already know each other? How can she ensure that the protégés will learn about her as a person, too, beyond her mentoring role?

Teacher to teacher: Aisha often asks protégés to find their place on a timeline, indicating when they had their first paid professional job in the early education field. Mira uses a similar approach by asking protégés to say how many years they have worked with young children. As they are sharing, she adds up all these years to demonstrate the collective years of knowledge about teaching, including her own, that are present within the group. Next, she asks protégés to indicate the roles they have filled in the field, such as assistant teacher, teacher, or family child care provider, and shares information about her own history. She then summarizes these results to

reinforce the experience and knowledge that resides among them. What other strategies might she use if protégés are very new to the field?

Learner to learner: Mira finds that asking her protégés to share about learning something new, such as using a new recipe, serves a twofold purpose. It's a great icebreaker, and it introduces the topic of how people approach learning. She also sometimes asks the protégés to try learning a new game, as in Chapter 2 activity. If all the protégés are teaching the same children, how might Aisha and Mira use a discussion about children's learning styles as a springboard for talking about their own approachs to learning?

Protégé to mentor: Aisha and Mira use the same process with groups of protégés as with individuals, asking protégés about what skills each of them would like to build, and new things they might want to try for the first time or approach differently in the classroom. It helps them understand the range of interests among the protégés, and to identify differences among protégés with respect to their comfort level in speaking up about their classroom practice. Do you think this is a productive approach? Can you think of any disadvantages? If so, what would you suggest as a better approach?

BEYOND FIRST IMPRESSIONS

You and your protégé will continue getting to know each other over the entire span of your relationship, ideally deepening the trust that makes it possible to offer both support and challenge in a mentor-protégé relationship. Sometimes, too, first impressions can be inaccurate, leading to false assumptions and miscommunication. Keep an open mind, and check yourself for snap judgments about your protégé. Be open to new information and interactions that could shift your initial impressions.

Getting to know your protégé better will involve developing a more in-depth assessment of her skills. Chapter 2 discussed how theory can provide a conceptual framework for understanding your protégé as an adult learner—but various theories can also help you assess your protégé's knowledge and skills related to teaching young children. Consider the stage theories of teacher development described on page 23:

- Is your protégé (in the novice or advanced beginner stage) concerned with issues of survival?
- Is she at the first stages of thinking about her ways of teaching?
- Does she have the words to describe why she approaches her teaching in particular ways?
- Would you describe your protégé as relatively advanced, competent in her skills, able to set goals, and focused on whether, how and what children are learning?
- Is she able to apply instructional techniques flexibly, based on children's individual needs?
- Is she sufficiently confident about her teaching that she is open to experimenting with new techniques?

There are no single correct answers to these questions, but the answers you arrive at can guide you in shaping learning experiences with your protégé that will be meaningful and relevant to her.

An accurate view of your protégé also involves paying attention to her work environment, which can either promote or inhibit her development as a teacher, much as the environment of an early childhood setting can promote or inhibit children's learning. Chapter 5 will discuss adult learning environments in greater detail, including tools you can use to assess them, but the following are some preliminary questions to assist you in thinking about your protégé's work and learning environment. Does this environment:

- provide adequate teaching supports such as:
  - a clearly identified curriculum framework;
  - a process for observing and assessing children;
  - sufficient and age-appropriate classroom equipment and supplies;
  - adequate numbers of staff to children;
  - consistent classroom, staff and child assignments; and
  - access to support services for children and families?
- offer opportunities for teachers to share ideas and learn from one another?
- encourage staff to explore new ideas about teaching?
- foster initiative and teamwork among teaching staff?
- support teachers' economic and physical well-being, by providing adequate compensation, health benefits, and paid sick leave and vacation?
- treat teachers fairly?

- include program leaders who are familiar with your protégé's teaching, knowledgeable about early childhood curriculum and teaching young children, and actively involved in learning themselves?

APPLYING YOUR COMMUNICATION SKILLS

Clear and sensitive communication is a cornerstone of any trusting relationship. The communication skills that you have honed over time in your work with young children, their families, and other colleagues will help you start off on the right foot with your protégé.

The practice of *active listening*—a form of communication commonly used by teachers with young children—can be particularly helpful in your relationship with your protégé. Active listening involves focused attention by the listener to what the speaker is saying, without interruptions, and with congruent body language, such as good eye contact, freedom from distraction, and an alert posture. Such attentiveness helps the person who is speaking to you feel acknowledged and taken seriously.

Once the speaker has paused or finished her comments, active listening also involves paraphrasing or "playing back" what you've heard. Summarizing in this way serves to further the conversation, and may even help the protégé resolve a challenging situation or clarify her thoughts.

To take one example: If a protégé says, "I can't figure out how to keep Kevin from hitting or pushing other children during art activities," a mentor might respond, "It sounds like Kevin is unhappy or frustrated in these situations; Have you noticed what happens right before he comes to the activity, or before he starts hitting or pushing? Have you tried to engage him in this type of activity one-on-one? Or just let him participate only when he chooses to?" In another instance, a mentor might say, "It sounds like you're finding transition times to be the most difficult part of your day. Can you tell me more about what makes them hard?" Rephrasing their concerns often helps protégés to form their own interpretations, draw their own inferences, and identify their own solutions. Active listening is more than a communication tool; it also offers your protégé a model of how to approach the problem-solving process, and to reflect on and assess her teaching practice.

Communication does not mean only talking and listening, of course; we also communicate by writing, watching, gesturing and moving. Mentoring involves being patient and attentive, recognizing all the forms of information that you and your protégé communicate in your meetings, as these, too, will inform the impressions you build about one another. Attend to how your protégé reacts to different situations, what she chooses to discuss or ask about, and her body language; any of these can offer insight into your protégé's concerns, and can help you target feedback appropriately.

Effective communication skills are essential to all types of teaching relationships and, ideally, continue to strengthen throughout all stages of your and your protégé's development. Resources listed at the end of the chapter, and several activities throughout the book, can help you and your protégé strengthen your communication skills.

APPRECIATING AND UNDERSTANDING DIFFERENCES

There are no hard-and-fast rules about what makes a good match between a mentor and a protégé. Mentors may or may not be older than their protégés, and may or may not have more years of experience in early care and education. If you are part of the same cultural community as your protégé, or have similar early care and education experience, these shared characteristics may make it easier for the two of you to get to know each other, although you should not take this for granted, since different experiences will have shaped your perspectives. But even if you are matched with a protégé with whom you have little in common, you can still build a close and trusting relationship. Mentoring an adult from a different cultural, racial or socioeconomic background requires the same kind of awareness you need to teach and care for young children from different backgrounds. Differences sometimes can stand in the way of understanding and communication, but they also can make relationships especially rich.

The concept of *cultural humility*, developed by trainers of medical professionals, can be helpful in building mutually respectful, dynamic and trusting relationships.[28] It starts with becoming conscious of your own cultural identity, defined here as the behaviors and beliefs characteristic of the particular group or groups with which you identify yourself (e.g., ethnicity, race, generation, gender, neighborhood, nationality). The idea behind cultural humility is that the more aware you are of your own assumptions and attitudes—those that emanate from your culture(s) or the groups you consider yourself a part of—the more likely you are to be both curious and nonjudgmental in learning about your protégé's cultural identities, and their implications for her beliefs and practices as a teacher.

In medical settings, the term "cultural humility" recognizes the power imbalance typically at play between patients and doctors or nurses, which can lead both parties to think only of the medical professional as an expert, even though patients are an important source of knowledge about themselves, their symptoms and their care. But humility is also an apt term when applied to adult learning relationships, serving to remind mentors and protégés about the contribution that each brings to the process, and to emphasize reciprocity. The term also signals a disposition toward continuing to learn about the cultures of others, but it is not the same as the more commonly used term, "cultural competence," which can be misinterpreted as meaning that the understanding of other cultures involves simply mastering a certain body of information. Of course, mentors and protégés can and should engage in building their knowledge about cultures and identities other than their own, but more importantly, you and your protégé will need to develop skills in raising questions, and discussing assumptions, that underlie different approaches to teaching and interacting with young children. For example: You may hold similar or different assumptions about feeding a toddler, vs. letting her feed herself, or the degree to which children of different ages should be expected to keep their clothing neat and clean, vs. being allowed to get dirty.

Underlying assumptions or beliefs may also influence how you and your protégé view your roles in relationship to each other. Some cultures view the teacher (or mentor) as a source of established knowledge that it's inappropriate to question, while others invite challenges to established points of view as integral to the learning process. Similarly, some may view it as a weakness to share professional challenges and problems, where others see the ability to articulate such challenges as an important step toward mastery. Uncovering such attitudes can help you clarify your communication, and find a comfortable balance between differing approaches.

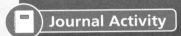

Journal Activity

Appreciating Differences as Learners

As you work together, it's important to recognize your protégé's level of confidence about learning, as it will affect how she responds to feedback. It's also important not to assume that just because a protégé is participating in a learning initiative, she feels confident about the process.

Ask your protégé to respond to the same journal questions you answered about your identity as a learner in Chapter 2, and the influences on this identity. Then exchange and compare what you've written. Your developing disposition toward cultural humility will be important for engaging your protégé in what may be a sensitive conversation about your identities as learners.

28. Tervalon & Murray-Garcia, 1998.

For more on issues of culture, bias, diversity and equity in the field of early education, see the list of References and Further Reading at the end of this chapter.

Journal Activity   Identity and Humility

Our own frameworks for understanding the world shape our behaviors toward other people. To approach others with cultural humility requires awareness of our own assumptions and expectations for relationships. For this activity, reflect in writing about your own identity, and the beliefs and values that influence your communications with others.

- How do you define your own personal cultural identity? Consider aspects of your identity that have been constant throughout your life, as well as those that may have changed over time. For example: your ethnicity, age, experience, education, socioeconomic status, gender, sexual orientation, religion, politics or other aspects of your identity.
- People are not always aware that their values and beliefs are not universally shared—particularly when they belong to a "dominant" group that leads many forms of discourse and sets the "norms" of behavior. Thinking

of your own values and beliefs, are there any that you consider "the norm"? If so, what impact might thinking in that way about your values have on your relationships with others who hold alternate viewpoints? For example, if you as a mentor believe that looking children in the eye when speaking with them is essential for appropriate teacher behavior, how might this assumption affect a protégé with different expectations about eye contact? Can you think of other aspects of teaching that may be influenced by personal or cultural values and beliefs? How might you engage your protégé in discussions about values and beliefs?

- Think of a situation in which you have felt different from most people. How did this make you feel? What, if anything, did others do that made you feel acknowledged and valued, despite differences among you? What, if anything, did they do that was hurtful or disrespectful?

? Questions for Discussion   "The Danger of a Single Story"

Drawing from her own life experiences, Nigerian author Chimamanda Ngozi Adichie illustrates how limiting and harmful it can be to have a "single story" about a person, community or country—in the way that this can emphasize differences and give rise to misunderstandings. In contrast, an openness to multiple stories promotes an understanding of similarities, and helps to move beyond stereotypes.

In preparation for, or during, a meeting with fellow mentors, listen to Adichie's 17-minute talk, "The Danger of a Single Story," available at http://www.youtube.com/watch?v=D9Ihs241zeg. Then consider the following questions:

- Is Adichie's notion of "the danger of a single story" familiar to you? Can you think of examples of "single stories" from the world of politics, entertainment or sports?

- Share an example of a single story that you think others may have about you. How does it influence how they respond to you? How has it shaped your view of yourself? How does it make you feel? What strategies have you used to move others beyond any single story about yourself?
- Share an example of seeing someone else through a single story. Do you know how you came to think about the person in this way? What has helped or could help you build a more multifaceted understanding of the person?
- What strategies can you use to ensure that you and your protégé see beyond single stories about each other?
- How might you use the idea of "the single story" when discussing children, parents or other teachers with your protégé?

In the five-minute video, "A Simple Trip to the Grocery Store," a woman talks about discriminatory treatment she encountered at a grocery checkout counter, why she didn't challenge the checker's behavior, and why and how her sister intervened to do so. Watch the video (available at http://world-trust.org/a-simple-trip-to-the-grocery-store) with your fellow mentors. Then consider the following questions:

- Have you ever been in a situation in which you and someone else were treated differently, or unequally, because of how you looked?
- Did both of you—the person treated disrespectfully and the one who was treated with respect—respond similarly? Why or why not?
- Discriminatory practices or inequitable treatment can occur in early care and education programs, as they can

in all institutions. In settings where you have worked as a teacher, have you ever witnessed discriminatory behavior or inequitable treatment because of someone's ethnicity, gender, religion, sexual preference or other aspects of cultural identity? How did you respond?

- Have you observed discriminatory or inequitable treatment or conversation in the programs where your protégés work? Have you chosen to comment on or interrupt the behavior? Why or why not? What was the result of your action or inaction?
- Has your protégé raised any issues about discriminatory behaviors toward children, co-workers or parents in her workplace? Or have you witnessed her engaging in such behaviors? Do you feel able to discuss issues of inequity or discrimination with her? How might you go about developing skills in this area?

BEGINNING YOUR WORK TOGETHER

Establishing ground rules early in your relationship with your protégé is as important as getting to know one another. You both share responsibility for the success of your relationship, and you are both making a commitment. Mentoring programs vary in their goals and objectives for protégés and how they view mentors' duties, but whatever your program's structure, you and your protégé will need to agree to:

- a format for your relationship, including when and where you will meet, and possible assignments between meetings;
- your communication rules, including how and when you will contact each other, establishing and meeting deadlines, and issues of confidentiality; and
- the specific protégé learning objectives that you will work on together.

At your first meeting, it may be helpful to begin by talking about learning objectives more generally, recognizing that it may take more than one session to come to an agreement on this part of your work plan. It may help to focus more attention at first on how you will meet and communicate, as these are likely to be more straightforward, and may even be clearly laid out by your mentoring program. Once you have agreed to the ground rules and work plan, it's useful to have a written contract or other document summarizing your decisions, to help prevent confusion or misunderstanding.

Setting Expectations: Finding Time and Space to Meet

In early care and education settings, it can be very challenging for teachers and other adults to find time to meet together. But mentoring relationships require regular, uninterrupted opportunities for conversation and planning. Time is critical in new relationships, and in learning to understand another person.

Mentor-Protégé Sample Agreement

Mentoring is a relationship-based form of professional development in which an experienced early childhood teacher supports the professional and personal capacity of a protégé. The specific goals of this mentoring program include:

I (mentor)_____ and I (protégé)_____
agree to work together from _____ (date) _____ to (date) _____.

As a mentor, I agree to:
- Work with my protégé on scheduling a consistent time at least _____ (frequency) _____ to visit her classroom;
- Help my protégé on developing goals for our work together and developing a work plan to meet those goals;
- Provide clear and supportive feedback on my protégé's teaching during conferences held (indicate frequency) _____;
- Support my protégé in learning new knowledge and skills;
- Remain open to developing my own knowledge and skills so that I can become a more effective mentor;
- Provide advice and share resources to help support the professional growth of my protégé;
- Come to our sessions prepared, having completed our agreed-upon tasks from our prior meeting together;
- Show up on time and provide advance notice if I am unable to visit my protégé's classroom during our scheduled time together;
- Treat our work together as confidential unless we have a clear written understanding of matters that can or will be shared with others. (My feedback will not be used as basis for my protégé's evaluation for continued employment. I am, however, required by law to report any suspicion of child maltreatment.)
- Have my protégé periodically evaluate her progress, our work together, and my performance as a mentor.

As a protégé, I agree to:
- Work with my mentor on developing learning and classroom goals and a work plan for our time together;
- Come to our sessions prepared, having completed our agreed-upon tasks from our previous session together;
- Engage in productive problem-solving with my mentor to identify ways to overcome any barriers that inhibit my professional growth and teaching practice;
- Show up on time, and provide advance notice if I am unable to make it to our mentoring session;
- Allow my mentor to observe in my classroom and meet with her to discuss my teaching;
- Periodically discuss my progress, our work together, and my mentor's work.

Signed_____ Date_____

Signed_____ Date_____

Ideally, during your first meeting, you and your protégé will develop a preliminary plan for conferencing and for visiting in the classroom. Which times will be most convenient, and how often will you meet? In some cases, the mentoring program will already have guidelines or parameters about what is expected, such as a prescribed minimum or maximum number of meeting hours. But even in such cases, it's important to be clear about how much time you need in order to have a productive and useful relationship.

Finding comfortable and private places for adults in early childhood programs can also pose a challenge. If you are meeting on site at an early childhood program, take some time before the initial meeting to identify appropriate meeting spaces in the building or nearby, such as a café. It's worth the extra effort to find a good physical environment where conversations between you and your protégé won't be interrupted or overheard. It is absolutely necessary

Distance Mentoring

Traditionally, when we think of mentoring, we envision face-to-face relationships: a mentor visiting a protégé's classroom, a protégé working alongside a mentor in the mentor's classroom, and the two parties meeting regularly to discuss their work. But advances in technology have also provided new ways for mentors and protégés to work together—leading to such terms as *distance mentoring, virtual mentoring, remote mentoring* or *telementoring*. In such arrangements, mentors and protégés rely on electronic tools such as videos, online chat or discussion rooms, telephones and e-mail.

Distance mentoring presents a unique set of opportunities and challenges. All effective mentoring relationships take time and planning, but it may take even more to establish trusting and effective relationships in long-distance arrangements. Spending time getting to know your protégé, connecting with her, asking her questions, and learning about the classroom and center in which she works, are all vital steps in creating a supportive climate for learning.

As a long-distance mentor, it will also be critical to establish regular communication with your protégé. Both of you should decide on the best lines of communication, whether by phone, e-mail, instant messaging, or other online contact, and the times that work best for both of you. Signing an agreement or contract that defines your level of commitment, including when, how and what you will communicate with each other, can help strengthen both parties' commitment to the relationship.

Many long-distance mentoring meetings are conducted over the phone. But most of us can all think of situations when we have been distracted during phone conversations, whether by a new e-mail that just popped up, or a conversation in the hallway. It's important to eliminate distractions—for example, shutting off your computer, and finding a quiet space—so

that you can pay extra attention to your protégé, listening actively during mentoring meetings. Visual cues that are available to us when meeting face-to-face will be absent, too, so you will also be sharpening your sensitivity to other kinds of cues, such as changes in tone of voice or pace of speech, and checking in frequently, perhaps by paraphrasing back to your protégé what you are hearing or understanding, to help avoid miscommunication.

Distance does not have to be a barrier in supporting your protégé's teaching and learning. Videos can be a very helpful mentoring tool for providing you and your protégé with material for reflection. Viewing videos of exemplary teaching practices together can be the basis for a variety of rich discussions, and will offer lasting images your protégé can draw on long after the mentoring relationship ends. And as your mentoring relationship progresses, your protégé may feel more comfortable videotaping her own teaching as a basis for discussion. Make sure that both you and your protégé have the technological tools you need.

As in all mentoring relationships, thorough preparation is critical to long-distance mentoring. To ensure that mentoring sessions are productive and focused on learning, you may find it helpful to follow a predictable routine. Begin, for example, by reviewing your protégé's last assignment, and asking her to reflect on what was successful, what she learned, how she thought children benefited, and what changes she would make. By the end of the conversation, agree on what the protégé will do in preparation for the next meeting, ask how she thinks this activity is connected to children's learning, and if possible, select tools that can support the assignment.

See "References and Further Reading" at the end of this chapter; the book by Zachary & Fischler (2009), for example, contains a section on long-distance mentoring.

that your protégé not be responsible for children during your meeting time, because splitting her attention between classroom responsibilities and her own learning will shortchange both efforts. If coverage issues arise unexpectedly, be prepared to reschedule your meeting.

It is important to identify who can assist you in making arrangements to facilitate meeting with your protégé. The director or principal at your protégé's place of work, or the coordinator of your mentoring program, for example, may be able to help arrange opportunities for you and your protégé to meet regularly, working out the details of classroom release time, substitute coverage, scheduling and other logistical matters. If you have difficulty finding time and a place for you and your protégé to meet, be sure to let this person know. If your protégé is a member of a union, check whether the contract addresses any agreements about meeting times.

As the relationship progresses, you and your protégé should check in regularly with each other about how well these time and space arrangements are working, and whether anything needs to be modified. Scheduling problems could occur for either or both of you.

Your agreements about meeting should also include clear expectations of what each of you will do between meetings. For example, you might agree to bring new materials or resources for your protégé; she might agree to develop a lesson plan to review at your next meeting; or you both might agree to watch a video or read something that you will discuss. Such "assignments" may emerge or change over time; nonetheless, it can be helpful to specify in your written contract or work plan that at the end of each meeting, you will confirm assignments for the next meeting.

Establishing How You Will Communicate

At the heart of developing a trusting mentor-protégé relationship is the commitment to be reliable to each other, and a good way to formalize such a commitment is to make a communication agreement. Agree to arrive on time to meetings, and to let each other know—perhaps with a specified amount of advance notice— whenever you need to make a change in your prearranged schedule. Since you and your protégé will probably be in communication between meetings, it's also useful to review how you will do that, whether through telephone calls, texting, Skype, or e-mail, as well as the best times for reaching each other.

Agree, too, to be clear and assertive in communicating with one another. Assertiveness is a way to be forthright and clear about your needs and wishes without manipulating or controlling others. An appropriately assertive person is skilled at using "I" statements to express feelings and needs directly, and to set limits and boundaries when necessary. A mentor might say, for example: "I know you prefer to meet on Tuesdays at 2 o'clock, but I'm finding it inconvenient—we're rushing our meetings a little so that I can pick up my son at school. Can we find another time that will work for both of us?"

Confidentiality is an essential part of establishing trust in a mentor-protégé relationship. Frankness and trust are only likely to develop when both partners know that the content of their discussions will not be shared with others. If any information is to be shared, you and your protégé will want to establish clear guidelines, specifying the types of information (possibly including observational assessment scores, or the mentor-protégé work plan), that can be shared with the protégé's supervisor, director or principal. Without such agreement, your protégé may be reluctant to talk about critical issues she is experiencing on the job that may be impeding her efforts to improve her teaching.

There is one important exception, however, to this policy of confidentiality. If a mentor or protégé comes to suspect that her partner's actions or practices may jeopardize the safety and well-being of children, she has a legal obligation to report these suspicions to the proper authority. All 50 states have enacted laws on reporting child abuse, precisely so that such harmful actions and practices are *not* kept secret. But in all other cases, you and your protégé should feel that you can share with each other, without worry, any doubts, questions and vulnerabilities you may have about teaching practice with young children.

Ideally, the communication plan will include a written agreement between your mentoring program and *the leadership at your protégé's workplace* (e.g., site supervisor, director, principal), spelling out the responsibilities of all parties: yours, the mentoring program's, your protégé's and those of the workplace leadership. The agreement should describe what you will and won't be doing; for example, "The mentor will observe her protégé at work in the classroom, and periodically demonstrate or model instruction with the children. She will not be asked to work in the classroom in lieu of adequate staffing or serve as the protégé's supervisor. Her role is to support the protégé in gaining new knowledge, practicing new skills and becoming more skilled in using instructional strategies to promote children's learning." Sometimes, however, directors may turn to mentors for help with supervising staff. In such a case, it's essential to clarify that supervision is not part of your role (see sidebar, "The Differences Between Mentoring and Supervision").

Sometimes, too, programs work with more than one mentor or coach at a time, and if feedback for teachers is not well aligned, confusion and frustration can arise for teachers and mentors alike. If you encounter a program that has multiple quality improvement efforts underway, ask the program leader to help clarify how these efforts are intended to work in tandem, to set guidance about priorities, and to resolve any differences in philosophy or approach.

The agreement between your mentoring program and your protégé's workplace leadership should also delineate expectations about time commitments, permissible changes in the classroom and confidentiality. For example, the agreement should describe the workplace's commitment to arranging a consistent time for the protégé to meet with her mentor, including some conferencing time away from children that allows her to focus exclusively on her own learning. Situations that need approval from the workplace leadership (such as the rearrangement of classroom space) should be clearly spelled out. Finally, the agreement should state the mentor's commitment to keep conversations with her protégé confidential—and should specify any allowable communication about their work together that either the mentor or the protégé may have with workplace leadership.

It is often a good use of your time to meet with leaders of your protégé's workplace early in the relationship. You can share the written agreement you've made with your protégé,

The Differences Between Mentoring and Supervision

A mentoring relationship is founded on peer support. Mentors are guides and role models who talk openly and directly with protégés about their work, help them improve their skills in interacting with children and families, and provide information and feedback. Mentors encourage protégés to take risks and meet new challenges, and help them develop their own professional goals. Mentors are open to learning, too—gaining insight from their protégés, attaining new skills, and reflecting on their own practices. Mentors do not function as supervisors, and do not conduct formal evaluations of their protégés.

Supervisors can be pedagogical leaders for teachers, and they can use many of the mentoring principles and strategies in this book to help employees do the best job possible. But a supervisor also has roles and responsibilities that interfere with a purely mentoring relationship—namely, the authority to fire, promote and make other decisions about a person's job status and livelihood. Mentors often do some assessment and evaluation of protégés, but not in a way that is linked to the protégé's continued employment.

Your primary role as a mentor will be to provide support and encouragement so that your protégé has someone to rely on and turn to. Trust is essential for a close relationship, along with willingness by both partners to reveal themselves and to risk making mistakes. A protégé is unlikely to reveal very much about herself if she is being evaluated in a way that could influence her future employment.

and also review portions of the larger agreement with your mentoring program that relate to your role.

Setting Goals: Agreeing to Work Together on Specific Learning Objectives and Outcomes

By the time you and your protégé are ready to decide on a work plan, ideally you will have discussed what she considers to be going well in her classroom, and how she would like to enhance and improve her teaching.

Sometimes, a protégé will find it difficult to articulate what she would like to change in her practice; in this situation, ask her to talk about one or two areas she finds particularly challenging, in which she would like to explore strategies that will enable her to feel more confident and competent. Many early care and education teachers are never asked about their teaching—why they do what they do—or encouraged to reflect about her practice. If this is true for your protégé, she may not yet know how to talk about what she would like to improve, and you will need to pose questions that help her begin to build these skills as an articulate practitioner.

Other protégés will speak more readily about their learning goals; this does not mean, however, that whatever your protégé wants to do will automatically determine the work plan. She may propose to work on something that is too narrow or too broad, and your job will be to help her expand or limit her scope in order to develop an agreement that is acceptable to the protégé and the mentor program alike.

In addition to the mentor-protégé agreement that delineates the responsibilities between you and your protégé, a "Protégé Learning Statement" can be used to set goals. Malcolm Knowles (Knowles, 1975; Knowles, Holton & Swanson, 2011) first articulated

Protégé Learning Statement

What am I trying to learn?	What strategies and resources will help me learn?	Over what period of time will I work on my learning objective(s)?	How will I measure my progress?	How will others verify my learning?	How will I build upon what I have learned?
Objective One:					
Objective Two:					
Objective Three:					

I have reviewed this learning statement.

Date: _____ Protégé: _____   Date: _____ Mentor _____

Activity | Setting Goals with Your Protégé

Role-playing can help you to experiment with strategies to use in goal setting, and to practice any approaches you have decided to use with your protégé. Below are two role-play situations. If you play the mentor role, how will you assess each situation? What might you say or suggest as next steps? If you play the protégé, consider your own history as a teacher, and whether you can remember how you might have responded in a similar situation. What would have been helpful to you? The role-playing can allow you to practice giving and receiving feedback, as you comment and react to your fellow mentors. If time permits, switch roles and play out the scenario that way. Be sure to leave time to give each other feedback.

Alternatively, if you don't have an opportunity to role-play or discuss goal-setting situations with others, use your journal. The writing process often helps to clarify your thinking about what is really at issue and how you might respond.

Situation 1: Julia recently completed her bachelor's degree in child development, and has opened a family child care home; Mira coaches her and other providers as they prepare for their Quality Rating and Improvement System (QRIS) review. When asked what she would like to work on, Julia says that her goal is to "make sure that all the 4-year-olds in my program are ready for kindergarten by the end of the school year." When Mira asks her to be more specific, Julia replies that she wants to help them strengthen their "executive functioning" and their numeracy skills. Asked to give examples of the underlying behaviors or skills associated with these terms, Julia says that these are important for "lifelong learning" and "closing the achievement gap." While Julia seems to know the "buzz words," she does not seem able to articulate what they mean.

Situation 2: Sharon's public school district always conducts formal assessments on the teachers. Historically, the ratings are shared with the mentor and the principal to help them in planning professional development for the teachers. She is not quite sure how to respond when one teacher, Yolanda, states that her goal this year is to raise her ratings by a full point. When asked about how she wants to focus her learning and professional development, Yolanda responds by talking about the changes she could make that would be most likely to boost her scores. She adds that she wants to focus on classroom organization, specifically the dimension related to ensuring a variety of learning modalities and materials in the classroom, noting, "This seems like a straightforward way to boost my numbers overall."

Situation 3: Another protégé of Sharon's has recently been reassigned from a second-grade classroom to a mixed-age classroom for 3- and 4–year-olds. An experienced teacher, she finds herself struggling to adjust to the emotional needs of her students, comforting crying children who have difficulty saying goodbye to their parents upon arrival and who break into tears frequently during the day. She complains to Sharon that she spends her day soothing and helping children manage their feelings rather than teaching.

Other situations: You and your fellow mentors may have examples of other situations that arise in the goal-setting process. Share your stories about what has or hasn't worked well, and try role-playing different probing questions for detecting your protégé's concerns and interests, as well as alternative strategies that can help move toward an agreement. Role-playing a protégé-mentor conference after the fact can be as helpful as rehearsing beforehand, offering an opportunity to explore alternative ways to handle situations you are likely to encounter in the future.

the idea of a self-directed approach for adult learners, to acknowledge the importance of greater independence and initiative-taking among adult learners. The statement, completed by the protégé, outlines how she would like to approach her learning process. (See the Protégé form below.) The statement addresses:

- What she would like to learn or accomplish;
- What strategies and resources, including her own skills and strengths, would help her learn;
- Over what period of time she would work on her learning objective(s);
- How she would measure her progress;
- How others would verify her learning; and
- How she would build upon what she has learned in the specified time period.

Sample Mentor-Protégé Work Plan

Objective: To deepen knowledge of instructional practices that support children's emergent literacy development and to create a classroom that fosters children's literacy skills. (Note: Sharon is the mentor, and Kayla is the protégé.)

GOAL	TASK	TIMELINE	OUR WORK TOGETHER
To gain a deeper understanding of children's language and literacy development	Read articles on emergent literacy.	Month 1	1. Sharon will locate relevant articles. 2. Sharon and Kayla will jointly read and discuss articles and meet weekly to discuss.
To understand markers of strong early literacy environments and to assess the current literacy environment in Kayla's classroom	1. Select and review a "classroom environment checklist" on literacy. 2. Conduct baseline review of literacy environment. 3. Use literacy environmental checklist to determine areas for improvement.	Month 2	1. Sharon will select a literacy-related "classroom environment checklist" to use, reviewing with Kayla the checklist's goals and how these are related to children's learning. 2. Both Sharon and Kayla will use the checklist to conduct a literacy environment review, then compare and discuss results. 3. Sharon and Kayla will identify areas for improvement related to children's literacy, and develop a new work plan around these areas.
To enhance children's understanding of story structure and to increase vocabulary knowledge	1. Select a group of stories with predictable plots to introduce in month 2. 2. Create story baskets for each child to be introduced as transition activity before lunch. 3. Introduce small-group shared reading time. 4. Create journals for children to dictate or write their version of the story that the group shared. 5. Create stage and prop baskets, and work with small groups to create scripts from journals to act out stories.	Months 2-5	1. Sharon and Kayla will observe in another teacher's classroom, and meet to discuss how that teacher has integrated shared story-time into her daily routines. 2. Sharon will co-lead small-group literacy time, and conference with Kayla; Kayla will begin leading as she feels comfortable.

GOAL	TASK	TIMELINE	OUR WORK TOGETHER
To enhance children's sight recognition of words, and to support their emergent writing skills	1. Create labels for classroom materials. 2. Develop a writing center. 3. During free play, scaffold children's dramatic play by introducing a grocery store shopping theme, then a post office theme, and facilitate making shopping lists, letter writing and reading.	Months 3-6	Sharon will work with Kayla on taking anecdotal notes, on what situations and behaviors to observe, and on using these notes to analyze children's learning over time.
To assess the literacy environment after working on improvement efforts, to better understand areas of growth and areas that still need improvement	Conduct another checklist review of the literacy environment.	Month 6	Sharon and Kayla will each use the checklist to conduct another literacy environment review, and will compare and discuss results, including areas of growth and areas to improve.

Some protégés will need more guidance in developing and modifying a goal statement than others, and for some programs, such as those with very prescribed learning objectives, or for some protégés, it may not be a suitable tool.

Next, making sure that you understand the goals and objectives of your mentoring program, and the degree of flexibility you have in interpreting them, is important to establishing a viable work plan with your protégé. Your program's goals may be intended more as a guide for your work with your protégé than as precise expectations of what you must do. On the other end of the spectrum, you might be dealing with specific learning expectations and outcomes established by your mentoring program that will be measured at the end of your work with your protégé. If you are unsure about the degree of flexibility you have with regard to determining your protégé's work plan, clarify these issues with your mentoring program coordinator or other authority. A successful mentoring partnership requires engaging your protégé actively in setting meaningful learning objectives.

Here, we provide a sample of a work plan developed by Sharon and her protégé Kayla; a blank template of this form can be found at the end of the chapter.

Setting Goals: Three Scenarios

At first glance, goal setting may seem straightforward. A protégé proposes what she would like to improve about her teaching, and the mentor makes some suggestions to focus the proposal and ensure that it is manageable. While this may sometimes be how it happens, mentors often find that the process requires more back-and-forth communication until an agreement is reached. Each of the following scenarios provides an example of issues that can arise in the goal-setting process.

Situation 1: Lori's mentoring program is linked to a community college's early child-hood lab school, and her protégés, who are relatively novice teachers, sometimes find it difficult to articulate specific goals. In such cases, Lori suggests that they observe other teachers, in order to generate ideas of skills they would like to develop or situations they want to learn to handle. When she began as a mentor, Lori was perhaps overeager to please her protégés, and often agreed too quickly to whatever goals they proposed. As her confidence and mentoring skills have developed, she now considers her protégés' suggestions as the first step in a give-and-take process.

Lori's protégé, Ella, works in the lab school two afternoons a week to fulfill the practicum requirement for a class on social-emotional development. At first, Ella said she couldn't think of anything to work on, but after visiting other classrooms, she proposes getting better at organizing classroom supplies.

Lori is somewhat surprised by the suggestion, because she has observed Ella already spending a lot of time "straightening up" the classroom, and reminding children to "put things where they go" and to "be careful not to make a mess." Using active listening, and sharing what she has noticed in a neutral way, Lori responds, "I hear that you value a well-organized classroom. I've also noticed when you work in the lab school that you like to keep things orderly. Can you tell me about how that helps you as a teacher, and the value of a well-organized classroom for children's learning?" Ella responds, "Children can't learn when things are messy, and teachers have to 'keep the lid' on the classroom." Lori realizes that she can take the conversation in two directions: how children learn or how teachers manage. She decides to follow the teacher thread, and asks Ella why keeping the lid on is important. Ella responds, "How will a teacher ever settle the children down if they get too wound up?"—and when pressed further, defines getting "too wound up" in terms of 4-year-olds talking loudly and moving too fast. Lori realizes that Ella doesn't yet have a firm grasp of what is common and non-worrisome behavior in 4-year-olds, and has limited strategies for engaging them when their enthusiasm and energy bubble over. Her strategy is to "keep a lid on," so that she won't find herself in situations she doesn't know how to handle.

Lori's task, as she sees it, is to shape a work plan with Ella that addresses her concerns about maintaining an orderly classroom, while guiding her to a broader understanding of children's normal social-emotional development, and learning the value of children's freedom of exploration and access to materials. She and Ella agree to work on developing classroom management skills around maintaining order and settling children down after an exciting activity, as well as observing more closely how children learn through both "order" and "mess."

Situation 2: Sharon works as a mentor in public school classrooms. This year, her work focuses on helping protégés implement a new approach to developing children's mathematical understanding. One protégé, Leslie, says that since her approach is to "follow the interests of the children," engaging them in projects that they choose themselves, she feels skeptical about "using a predetermined curriculum." Rather than arguing or becoming defensive, Sharon asks Leslie about her previous experience with such curricula. Leslie describes a "very academic" curriculum that the school district selected two years ago and later discontinued, and says emphatically, "I'm not interested in what children *should* know, but in how to promote their curiosity." Sharon responds that available curricula vary considerably in content and emphasis; she agrees that some can be very directive, even rigid, but others serve more as a guide for teachers.

Having acknowledged Leslie's concern, while suggesting that some curricula have more value than others, Sharon turns the discussion to numeracy: What are the areas of mathematical understanding that Leslie is hoping to work on this year, and what classroom strategies does she have in mind? Leslie mentions a post office project the children are excited about, which she sees as a good opportunity for extending children's understanding of measurement: describing measurable properties (length, weight, size), using words to compare these properties (bigger or smaller, shorter or longer), ordering objects by measuring them (shortest to longest) and trying different measuring tools.

Sharon agrees that the postal project could be an excellent way to meet her learning goals, and suggests that they look at the curriculum together for any ideas or activities to help Leslie meet her goals. To Leslie's surprise, she finds several ideas to try, and she and Sharon develop a work plan that uses the curriculum but applies it in the context of the learning program that Leslie wants to pursue. They also agree to explore the ways in which a "child-centered" approach is enhanced by teachers' guidance. While Leslie is still not completely sold on the curriculum, she's willing to explore how it might be adapted to fit with her theme. They agree to revisit the work plan in several weeks.

Situation 3: Mira is a coach who works with a Quality Rating and Improvement System. Her new protégé, Tara, shows a strong tendency to blame classroom problems on others, whether it's parents who "don't discipline their children," the "bad attitude" of the director or her co-teachers, or even the children themselves. In response to being asked what she would like to work on, Tara repeatedly says such things as, "If so and so would only _____, everything would be fine." She seems unable to reflect on her own role as a teacher. Mira realizes that her task involves getting Tara to think about herself as an actor in her classroom, and to recognize what she can and cannot control.

Mira begins by acknowledging how hard it can be to work with other adults; she herself has struggled with the give-and-take in early childhood classrooms that have more than one teacher, particularly because her college ECE program, like many others, paid little attention to helping build her skills in working with adults. Tara acknowledges that she, too, has had no training in this area, and her demeanor softens as she begins to see that her challenges are not unique. Mira asks, "Imagine for a moment that you don't have other teachers to deal with"—both of them laugh a bit—"what would you like to be working on?" Tara sighs and says, "I never think about that. I suppose I'd like to work on the transitions between activities. We all seem to be going in opposite directions." Mira notes that while Tara has mentioned the other teachers again, she has included herself this time. Mira responds only to the topic of transitions, however, asking Tara to say more about what she thinks works and doesn't work. They agree that Mira will observe the transitions in Tara's classroom during the next visit, as the starting point for the work plan.

Activity

Practice Developing a Work Plan

The above scenarios demonstrate a variety of challenges that mentors may face, and strategies they might use, in helping protégés set goals. Now, select one or more of the scenarios, and practice developing a work plan of your own. The Sample Mentor-Protégé Work Plan in this chapter can serve as a guide.

Mira recognizes that getting to the bottom of the dynamics at play between Tara and other staff will only happen gradually over the course of their work together. But for now, she has succeeded in establishing a starting point for talking with Tara about her own teaching. When Mira next meets with all the protégés in Tara's classroom, she will introduce activities organized around the issue of transitions, so that the team can work on listening and communication skills with each other, as well as strategies for negotiation and compromise.

* * * * * *

Now, having gone through the process of developing a work plan, it's time to put that plan into action. The following chapter focuses on skills and strategies to help you and your protégé work effectively together and reach your goals.

Mentor-Protégé Work Plan Template

Overall Objective(s):

GOAL	TASK	TIMELINE	OUR WORK TOGETHER
1.		Start: _____ End: _____	
2.		Start: _____ End: _____	
3.		Start: _____ End: _____	
4.		Start: _____ End: _____	
5.		Start: _____ End: _____	
Due to the varying duration of mentor programs, intervals between meetings or activities may span days, weeks or months. Insert appropriate intervals for your program.			

REFERENCES AND FURTHER READING

Delpit, L. (1995). *Other people's children: Cultural conflict in the classroom*. New York: The New Press.

Derman-Sparks, L., & Ramsey, P. (2006). *What if all the children are white?* New York: Teachers College Press.

Derman-Sparks, L, & Phillips, C. B. (1997). *Teaching/learning anti-racism: A developmental approach*. New York: Teachers College Press.

Donoghue, P. & Siegel, M. (2005). *Are you really listening?: Keys to successful communication*. Notre Dame, IN: Ava Maria Press.

Espinosa, L. (2009). *Getting it RIGHT for young children from diverse backgrounds: Applying research to improve practice*. Saddle River, NJ: Prentice Hall.

Garavuso, V. (2009). *Being mentored: Getting what you need*. New York: McGraw-Hill, Practical Guide Series.

Garner, R. (2011). *Constructing effective criticism: How to give, receive, and seek productive and constructive criticism in our lives*. The Woodlands, TX: Prescient Publishing.

Gay, G. (2000). *Culturally responsive teaching: Theory, research and practice*. New York: Teachers College Press.

Guilar, J. (2001). *The Interpersonal Communication Skills Workshop: Listening, assertiveness, conflict resolution, collaboration*. New York: American Management Association.

Gutierrez, K. & Rogoff, B. (2003). Cultural ways of learning: Individual traits or repertoires of practice. *Educational Researcher, 32,* 19-25.

Knowles, M. S. (1975). *Self-directed learning: A guide for learners and teachers*. Englewood Cliffs, NJ: Prentice Hall/Cambridge.

Knowles, M.S., Holton, E. F., III & Swanson, R. A. (2011). *The adult learner: The definitive classic in adult education and human resource development* (Seventh ed.). Burlington, MA: Elsevier.

Lynn, A. (1998). Long-distance mentoring guidelines for success. Retrieved at http://www.lynnleadership.com/distance_article.htm.

President and Fellows of Harvard College (1999). *Harvard Business Review on effective communication* (Ninth edition). Cambridge, MA: Harvard Business School Press.

Singleton, G. & Linton, C. (2006). *Courageous conversations about race: A field guide for achieving equity in schools*. Thousand Oaks, CA: Crowing Press.

Tannen, D. (1995). "Waiting for the mouse: Constructed dialogue in conversation." In *The dialogic emergence of culture*, eds. B. Mannheim & D. Tedlock, 198-217. Philadelphia: University of Pennsylvania Press.

Tervalon, M. & Murray-Garcia, J. (1998). Cultural humility versus cultural competence: A critical distinction in refining physician training outcomes in multi-cultural education. *Journal of Health Care for the Poor and Underserved, 9*(2), 117-125.

Zachary, L. & Fischler, L. (2009). *The mentor's guide: Facilitating effective learning relationships*. San Francisco: Jossey-Bass.

Chapter 4

Creating Change:
Skills and Strategies for Effective Mentoring

Having a particular skill—even if we are highly proficient at it—doesn't necessarily mean that we can pass it on to someone else. Being a great baker or cook is probably a prerequisite for hosting a TV cooking show, but it certainly doesn't guarantee high ratings. The successful television chef doesn't just demonstrate her skills; she can describe what she's doing as she goes, taking us through the steps in an accessible way. The clarity and style of her actions and explanations are what draw us in as viewers.

So, too, with a good early childhood mentor. Mentors are *articulate practitioners*[29]—able not only to demonstrate excellent skills with young children, families and other adults in the early learning environment, but to talk about their skills and practices meaningfully with others. By bringing your own thinking and practice to light, you help your protégés to become more articulate practitioners themselves.

To take one example: You can demonstrate how you facilitate children's numeracy or pre-math skills as they "play store" in the dress-up corner—*and* you can explain the thinking behind your words and actions, as well as why you may have rejected other possible strategies. In doing so, you not only provide direct experience and information for your protégé, but you also are modeling the cognitive and decision-making processes that underlie good teaching and its connection to how children learn. Your foundational knowledge about, and experience with, children and pedagogy are your tool kit.

BECOMING AN ARTICULATE PRACTITIONER

Many good teachers are unconsciously competent; they can't always articulate why they do what they do. But to be an effective teacher of teachers, a mentor must become consciously competent,[30] so that she can bring her own process to light for her protégé to consider. You can also articulate to your protégé the *limits* of your knowledge and experience, and offer to explore a topic of interest together with her: "I don't know much about supporting children's early math skills, but I know of a recent book on the subject; let's read it and talk about it." Such an admission of your own limits communicates that teacher development is continuous, even for teachers who are considered "advanced," and it shows the protégé that teaching challenges are also opportunities.

For your protégé, cultivating self-awareness about teaching may be a relatively new experience. Much of your task is to instill a sense of trust through close communication—sharing your own openness to reflecting on your own activities and practices as a teacher, and offering tools for growth, many of which we'll address in this chapter. A reflective, articulate practitioner:

- Is able to identify new ways of doing daily routines and activities;
- Grows in understanding of how and why she does what she does in the classroom;
- Learns from unsuccessful activities or experiences, adjusts her practice, and tries new approaches;

---

29. Takanishi, 1980.
30. Roll, Aleven, McLaren & Koedinger, 2007.

- Realizes the need to ask for help when uncertain about how to handle a situation or problem;
- Plans strategies for improvement, and sets goals to achieve them; and
- Recognizes her accomplishments, and builds on what works best.

Mentoring is a process of helping a protégé to improve and deepen her teaching practice, a way of creating growth and change—and as such, it means that mentors offer protégés not only *support*, but *challenge*.[31] When working with young children, a teacher creates a nurturing and safe environment, but at the same time, she challenges children to try new things, and opens up new possibilities. So, too, with protégés: you are helping to enlarge their vision and practice of teaching. And just as children differ in their readiness for and response to change and growth, some protégés may be more open or more resistant than others. This chapter focuses on skills you need, and strategies you can use, for creating change.

There are a variety of tools at your disposal. While you will not use all of them in every instance, or in this order, we present them here with one strategy leading to the next, and conclude with taking stock of your progress and setting new goals, as the cycle begins again. Strategies for mentoring are not a one-time process. Just as you do when you are working with young children, you are continually observing and getting to know your protégé, assessing her stage of learning and development, reassessing your own needs for further learning, and continually revising your goals, along with the choice of strategies and tools you will use to reach them.

Keeping a log of your contacts with your protégé (see Mentor Feedback Form at the end of this chapter) is helpful for charting changes you notice in your protégé over time. You can also use it as a form of self-assessment, noting the strategies you use or don't use, and reflecting on ways you could have handled a particular situation differently.

 **Activity** Assessing Yourself as an Articulate Practitioner

Use the following chart to reflect on your teaching skills with children, as well as your skills in *articulating* how and why you teach in particular ways.

First, assess your strengths in a variety of areas in which you may be called upon to help your protégé ("doing"). If you consider yourself highly skilled as a teacher in an area, mark 1. If you have some knowledge but do not consider yourself advanced in an area, mark 2. For areas in which you have very limited or no knowledge, mark 3.

Then, for each item, consider your strengths and skills in *articulating* your teaching approaches ("explaining"). If you consider yourself highly skilled in articulating your teaching approach in a particular area, mark 1. If you consider yourself moderately able to explain your teaching in a particular area, mark 2, and if you consider yourself unable to do so in a particular area, mark 3. This chart can be used in two ways: It can guide your own professional development, and it can also help you (and your mentoring program) determine whether you are an appropriate match for particular protégés.

31. Daloz, 1999.

Teaching Children and Mentoring Adults: Doing and Articulating

Content	BIRTH THROUGH 2 YEARS		3 YEARS THROUGH PRE-K		KINDERGARTEN THROUGH GRADE 3	
	Doing	Explaining	Doing	Explaining	Doing	Explaining
Promoting mathematical thinking and skills						
Promoting scientific thinking						
Promoting literacy						
Promoting artistic experiences						
Teaching about culture and community						
Using play in the curriculum						
Supporting and extending children's physical skills						
Supporting children's social development						
Planning and implementing integrated curriculum						
Supporting children with challenging behaviors in the classroom						
Teaching children with special needs						

Content	BIRTH THROUGH 2 YEARS		3 YEARS THROUGH PRE-K		KINDERGARTEN THROUGH GRADE 3	
	Doing	Explaining	Doing	Explaining	Doing	Explaining
Integrating children with special needs into the classroom						
Teaching children from diverse cultural, ethnic, and economic backgrounds						
Teaching children who are dual language learners						
Observing, assessing, and documenting to inform teaching and learning						
Classroom management						
Building relationships with other teachers and/ or other early childhood professionals						
Working with families						
Identifying community resources						

OBSERVATION AND CONFERENCING

Effective teachers spend time reflecting about their classroom experiences with young children, and they also become progressively more adept at adjusting their usual practices to best fit the needs of a child or group of children in a given situation. This may mean altering a planned activity in favor of an unforeseen learning opportunity—what educators often call a "teachable moment." It could mean jumping ahead to a later part of the activity or unit because the children are ready to progress more rapidly, or because they are interested in different aspects of the subject than those that had sparked the interests of a previous group. Through mentoring, this ability to be a flexible, constantly evolving practitioner—to "think on your feet"—is enhanced by a regular practice of observation and conferencing, a process that allows you and your protégé to reflect on effective teaching approaches together.

Observing your protégé at work in the classroom, like observing children at play, is a potentially powerful source of information. Your observations may be global at first, as you form an impression of how your protégé interacts with children individually and as a group; how she organizes the classroom or introduces activities; the frequency, duration and tone of her communications with other staff and with parents; and her overall sense of comfort and confidence in her role. This process may also include the use of structured observation tools (see "Using Structured Observation Tools," later in this chapter).

An observation and conferencing process might include the following sequence:

Step 1. Based on the work plan, the mentor and protégé meet to share information about what they want the observation to focus on: for example, handling transition times, or large group activities. They set a time for the observation, and the mentor asks what the protégé would especially like her to look for. They agree upon an observation or assessment tool to use, or key questions to address.

Step 2. The mentor observes the protégé, for a set period of time, in a given activity or interaction with a child or group of children.

Step 3. The mentor and protégé meet in conference to discuss the observation—perhaps immediately, or later that day, or within the following week, but not letting too much time elapse between observation and discussion. They reflect together on what was observed, and how the protégé feels the activity or interaction went. The mentor asks questions and gives feedback, describing what she saw and/or didn't see. She might ask, for example: How did you feel about the activity? Why? How would you describe what happened with the children? Did your behavior or strategies differ in any way from what you had planned? If so, how or why did you make different decisions? Did you achieve your goals, and how do you know this? Is there anything you would do differently next time? (See "Giving and Receiving Feedback," later in this chapter.)

Step 4. At the end of the conference, the mentor and protégé determine some goals for the coming period of time, and set another observation date. This time they may identify new areas to observe that relate to whatever new goals are set.

Step 5. A second observation takes place, and the cycle is repeated.

MODELING

Modeling is another name for demonstrating skills, methods or practices to protégés—a way of teaching by showing a skill, not simply describing it. As a strategy, modeling should be followed up with conversation, so that the mentor and protégé can talk about what has taken place, and how to adapt this approach to the protégé's own situation. The point is not that you are demonstrating the "correct way" of approaching a particular teaching situation, or that your protégé should simply copy your teaching style, but that you are showing her possibilities for change.

Perhaps your protégé is a teacher who thinks that art activities with children should be geared toward making or drawing lifelike or easily recognizable representations. You might start by observing her work with small groups of children to see how she introduces such activities. You may notice that she always asks children to tell her what they are painting, and directs their easel painting by suggesting where they should add a mouth to a face or a tail to an animal, instead of considering that children may have no specific object in mind when drawing and painting, but may have learned to provide "the right answer" to satisfy adults' request for a label.

Before you ask your protégé to try a different approach, you may try modeling other kinds of conversations with children about their art work—asking, for example, "Tell me something about your painting," to further a discussion rather than seek a particular answer. You might introduce a free-form art activity in which you provide materials for children to create whatever they choose about a particular topic, such as fall colors and textures, rather than pumpkin cutouts. Instead of suggesting outright that your protégé change her approach, you are indicating an alternative that can serve as the springboard for conversations and possible changes later on. The first step is for your protégé to become aware of other options for an activity she might do routinely; in time, she may reach a greater understanding of and openness to different approaches, develop a deeper grasp of art as a form of expression, and engage in richer conversations with children.

JOURNALS AND OTHER WRITING

Writing presents another opportunity for thinking about and expressing our questions and challenges about teaching, and to describe our practices with children and the reasons behind them. For the protégé, it can help in becoming more conscious and articulate in her teaching practice. For you as a mentor, journals and other writing assignments can enhance your understanding of your protégé's knowledge and skill.

To develop appropriate writing assignments for protégés, you will need to consider their varying levels of skill and comfort with writing. Some may find it difficult because of issues of literacy. If English is a protégé's second language, it is particularly important to ask whether she prefers to read and/or write in her native language. And, of course, some protégés will benefit more if they can communicate orally with a mentor in their home language.

Keeping a journal is good way for a teacher to become more consciously competent through writing practice. We have been offering suggestions for you, as a mentor, to keep a journal about many of the topics under discussion in this book. A journal can be equally useful for a protégé. It can remain private, or the protégé can choose to share some or all of its contents. A journal can be an open-ended, free-form, daily or weekly exercise, as the protégé seeks to record her classroom experiences, questions or challenges—or you and your protégé can agree on topics or questions to write about in the journals, to discuss later when you get together.

Other writing assignments are often appropriate for exploring topics or questions of early care and education practice in greater depth:

- *Creating written lesson plans* is a fruitful area to work on together, whether or not this activity is already a familiar part of a protégé's job. (See the sample lesson plan and evaluation form on this page.)
- *Observations of children.* To enrich a discussion of a particular child your protégé is finding challenging, ask her to conduct one or more written observations of the child in the course of the day, perhaps for five to 15 minutes, and in different types of activities. Ask

her, when observing, to set aside judgments or preconceptions as much as possible, and simply to record what she sees and hears, as objectively as she can—for example, the child's activities, movements and interactions with others, and what he or she says. Such an observation could also focus on two or more children for a certain period of time. Use these records in conferencing with your protégé, as part of your ongoing assessment of the child's or children's learning needs and of approaches the protégé can try.

- *Reflecting on activities with children.*[32] Choosing a particular activity, ask your protégé to write about how and why she took certain approaches, how she understands the results, and what she might try differently next time. The lesson plan form on the next page is also a questionnaire form that can serve as a framework for such reflection.

GIVING AND RECEIVING FEEDBACK

The art of giving and receiving feedback in a mentor/protégé relationship isn't always easy. Especially at first, a protégé may feel inexperienced or sensitive about learning from a veteran about ways to improve her teaching practices. You, as a mentor, might be just learning about how to offer help and suggestions for change, and you might sometimes fumble. Remembering that it's a two-way street will help you to work out supportive methods for communicating, without some of the tension that frequently accompanies traditional evaluations by supervisors.

As we have noted throughout this chapter, your role as a mentor is to offer both support and challenge, in the interest of helping your protégé grow in her teaching practice with young children. Above all, the most useful feedback is specific. If you have been observing your protégé in the classroom, what did you see and not see? What did you hear? What was the tone and quality of teacher interactions? How does this link to children's learning? Keeping your responses child-focused—rather than focused on the protégé as a person—can make it much easier for the protégé to receive feedback about something that didn't go well or that could be better. (For example: "Simon and Lucy seemed to be having a hard time during the story circle; let's talk about what might work better next time for keeping them engaged.") Keep in mind that, at least at first, it might be hard for your protégé to hear anything but the challenging or "negative" parts of your feedback. Especially when offering difficult feedback, it's important to remain compassionate and supportive, considering your protégé's individual style of communication, and adjusting your style accordingly.

Remember, also, that even positive feedback can be challenging to receive. Since your protégé may have a difficult time accepting praise, be sure to keep praise specific, too—neither overpraising nor resorting to generalities like "good," "great" and "excellent." (For example: "I noticed how well you redirected Sam to a different activity; it really helped him get out of a frustrating situation.") Praise should be encouragement, but it's also a form of instruction, a way of clarifying good practice as well as the goals you are seeking to reach together.

After an observation (see "Observation and Conferencing"), solicit feedback from your protégé herself about how the activity went: how she would describe what happened, what strategies she used, what worked well and what didn't, whether she felt she had achieved her goals, and what she might do differently next time. She may be aware already, at least in general terms, of the ways in which she needs and wants to improve and grow, all of which gives you a lead-in to offer your own responses. Perhaps you will also have used an audio or video recording of the activity, allowing the two of you to view an "objective" record of it together.

---

32. Schön, 1983.

Lesson Plan Template

Activity Name and Description:
Location and Date:
Materials needed, and how they will be introduced:
Developmental domain(s) that the lesson will address: 　　　　　____ Gross motor 　　　　　____ Fine motor 　　　　　____ Cognitive 　　　　　____ Perceptual 　　　　　____ Social/emotional 　　　　　____ Language
Specific concepts or skills to be addressed within these domain(s):
Instructional strategies (what you as a teacher will do to facilitate learning):
Adaptations (how to include individual children, e.g. English language learners, children of varying developmental levels, children with special needs):
AFTER THE ACTIVITY
Children involved:
Briefly describe what happened: How did the child(ren) approach the materials? Give examples of how you emphasized different developmental domains. Give examples of how you appropriately adapted the activity for the children involved.
Do you think this activity was valuable for the children's growth and development? Why or why not?
How did you feel about the way this activity went? Why?
How would you change (narrow, adapt, build on) this activity if you were to try it again?

Activities | **Giving and Receiving Feedback**

1. Lori, a mentor teacher whose classroom is a field placement site for early childhood education students, has been observing her protégé Karen conducting teacher-led activities with a group of 3-year-olds. Her overall impression is that Karen's activities are lasting too long, and require too much quiet sitting and attention from the children. This morning at the story circle, Karen read to them for over 10 minutes from a book with relatively few pictures, which she was able to show only intermittently because there was a great deal of text to read. Well before she had finished reading the story, Karen became irritable and impatient with the children's growing restlessness, and soon began raising her voice, even threatening to take away some free-play time if the group did not settle down and pay better attention. Their transition to the next activity was difficult and tense.

Lori and Karen both enjoy this particular book, and had even discussed the choice in advance. How might Lori give feedback to Karen about how the activity went, when they meet for a conference this afternoon?

2. A growing number of videos of teachers in early education classrooms are available, many of them online. Consult your mentor program, local child care resource and referral agency, or state department of education, for possible video sources. For videos highlighting social-emotional development, visit the Vanderbilt University Center on the Social and Emotional Foundations for Early Learning site at http://csefel.vanderbilt.edu. Watch one or more scenes with fellow mentors, or with a protégé. Then, take turns practicing giving appropriate, specific and helpful feedback to that teacher, explaining the reasons for your particular approach.

Finally, you can model how to receive feedback yourself, soliciting responses from your protégé about how or whether you have been helpful as a mentor, and what you might do differently, rather than waiting for this to "just happen" spontaneously. This is another critical part of building trust, mutuality and respect. Ask, for example: Has my feedback to you been helpful? Specific enough? Supportive? Appropriately challenging? Encourage your protégé to give specific examples in her feedback, just as you aim to do in your feedback to her. In cases where your assistance may be falling short, you may also be able to find further resources and information together: see "Reading and Research," page 58.

USING STRUCTURED OBSERVATION TOOLS

In addition to the kinds of classroom observation we've been describing, a number of structured observation tools, scales and checklists are often used in the early care and education field today, and are commonly linked with assessment, scoring, and/or evaluation. Many mentors work within quality improvement projects that use standardized assessments in order to rate quality in classrooms and family child care homes. Some assessments focus more on the overall classroom environment, while others focus more on the teachers.[33] (See box, "Examples of Structured Observation Tools.") Other tools may be related to a state's early education teacher competencies, or children's learning standards.

Some mentoring programs may require you to conduct a structured observation using one of these tools, or to use the results from an assessment conducted by someone else, as the basis for your work with your protégé. If you are relying on an assessment conducted by someone other than you, it is important to augment the report by collecting your own first-hand information, observing your protégé as she teaches.

Classroom and teacher assessments can offer you and your protégé important data about how your protégé structures her classroom, the instructional areas in which she

---

33. Halle, Vick Whittaker & Anderson, 2010.

Giving and Receiving Feedback in the Context of Differences in Language, Age, Education and Culture

1. Sharon's protégés are head teachers working with 4-year-old children in public school classrooms. Her protégé Beth, a Caucasian who speaks English only, works in a classroom of mostly Latino, Spanish-speaking children; Beth's assistant teacher, Lupe, a Spanish-speaking Latina, lives near the school and frequently sees some of the children and their parents outside of school hours in the neighborhood. As a result, Lupe often serves as the "go-to" teacher for parents when they have information to share or questions to ask about their children. As head teacher, Beth finds the situation troubling, and recently asked Lupe to refrain from chatting, beyond saying hello, when parents drop off or pick up their children. Beth knows that she caused offense by making this request, reporting that Lupe "got very quiet." Beth knows she has difficulty in communicating with the parents, but is also frustrated, and worried that Lupe is undermining her authority. "Lupe's relationship with the parents hasn't changed," Beth says, "but now she seems very formal with me, less friendly than she was before."

Sharon knows that cultural dynamics among teaching staff can affect the climate of the classroom, and sees that a first step is to help Beth become aware of this. While Beth is reasonably skilled in talking about cultural dynamics among the children, she has avoided any direct acknowledgment of differences or tensions with her adult peers. Sharon's goal is to help Beth and Lupe engage in a different kind of conversation about the differences in their linguistic and cultural backgrounds. She hopes they can come to see these differences as enriching rather than diminishing each other's teaching, as well as the experiences of the children and the parents. She also hopes that as Beth becomes more secure in her role, she will broaden her view of Lupe as "just a helper," and see her more as a co-teacher who makes important contributions to the classroom and serves as a role model for the children.

If you found yourself in a situation similar to Sharon's, what outcome(s) would you hope for? Which of the following issues might you raise with your protégé? Are there other approaches you would try?

- It sounds uncomfortable between you and Lupe. How might the tension be affecting the children?
- Can you share a little more about how this situation with Lupe makes you feel about your own teaching?
- We agree that it's important for parents to be able to share information about their children. What strategies can we pursue to help you build your relationship with the parents?

Are there any opportunities, along with the challenges, of having Lupe as an assistant teacher? If so, how might you build on these?

2. Aisha's responsibilities include conducting training workshops on a science curriculum with teams of protégés from several classrooms at a time. She finds it easy to establish rapport with some protégés, but difficult with others. Sometimes, she feels that she is "losing control" of a training session, especially when protégés start talking among themselves. In discussing her situation with a fellow mentor, Aisha realizes that she has an easier time with protégés she considers her peers: college-educated women in their late 20s or 30s. Many of her protégés, however, are as old as or older than her parents, and many of the older protégés do not have college degrees. In describing the situation, Aisha realizes that she feels intimidated by older protégés—particularly because, even though she has more education, many of these women have much more experience with children. "When they talk among themselves," she tells her colleague, "I assume that they're criticizing me, waiting for me to make a mistake. I feel like I used to feel when I invited my mother and aunt to try my cooking."

But Aisha is tired of "walking on eggshells" and wants to name what is going on. She realizes that older, more experienced protégés may have some cause to be skeptical about what she has to offer—and also that she may have a lot to learn from them. At the same time, she believes that the science curriculum can be helpful to them, and she is skilled at helping teachers learn how to adapt it to their needs. In part, she thinks that talking about these issues directly would be a relief, and could help everyone get more out of their time together. But she also is worried it could backfire, making it even more difficult for her to conduct the trainings and work effectively with the protégés.

If you found yourself in Aisha's situation, what would you do? Would you raise these differences in age or educational background? How? What could be gained by doing so? Are there risks involved in raising these issues, and are there risks in remaining silent? If you decided to raise these issues, would you do it one-on-one, or with the group as a whole?

Have you ever faced a situation arising from differences among the adults with whom you work? What was the outcome? What did you learn that might help you in assisting a protégé to navigate and grow in situations involving dynamics related to differences in culture, age, class, language or job role?

is strong, and areas that may need improvement. This information can be a useful launching point for talking with your protégé about her practice, and for selecting aspects of it that the two of you will work on together. Classroom assessments also are helpful for gauging progress and changes in your protégé's practice over time. But just as a teacher of young children may use a developmental checklist to frame her understanding of a particular child, but also will rely on other observations and interactions to inform her overall assessment, it is important to supplement results from formal assessments with additional data.

Classroom and teacher assessments may seem to be very abstract to your protégé; it may not be clear to her how the classroom characteristics or teaching practices they measure actually support children's learning and development. An important role you can play is to "translate" such assessments by helping your protégé consider why particular practices or classroom features are being measured, and how these relate to high-quality early education.[34] In the process, assessment tools can be a way of helping your protégé articulate what she does in the classroom, and why. By engaging your protégé in such discussion, she can begin to consider these tools more as a learning resource than just an assessment method or "report card."

? Questions for Discussion

As part of her coaching program, which is connected with a Quality Rating and Improvement System, Mira receives a report before she meets with a new protégé, including the protégé's scores on two different standardized assessments. But occasionally, such reports arrive after she has met with the new protégé and observed her teaching. Recently, Mira has concluded that her relationships with new protégés can get off on a better footing when she doesn't receive assessment scores in advance. She feels that she's then more open to forming her own opinions of her protégés' strengths and weaknesses, and that protégés can be more relaxed and open when scores, per se, are not the initial focus of conversation. One of her fellow coaches disagrees, however, and likes having as much information as possible in advance, feeling that these reports do not sway her thinking about new protégés.

What might be some pros and cons for a coach or mentor to have access to observation and assessment scores before meeting with a protégé? For waiting to view such scores until after a meeting? How could these two approaches affect the protégé? The coach or mentor?

Examples of Structured Observation Tools

The *Environment Rating Scales* are focused on the overall quality of a setting, and assess items such as the physical environment, daily schedule, personal care routines, safety, language stimulation, interactions among children and teachers, and curricular materials and activities. There are separate scales for preschool classrooms (ECERS-R: Harms, Clifford & Cryer, 1998), infant-toddler classrooms (ITERS-R: Harms, Cryer & Clifford, 2003), and family child care homes (FCCERS-R: Harms, Cryer & Clifford, 2007).

The *Classroom Scoring and Assessment System*, or CLASS (Pianta, 2003; Pianta, La Paro & Hamre, 2008; La Paro, Hamre & Pianta, 2012) is specifically designed to examine teaching practices. Items on the CLASS focus on the emotional climate of the classroom (e.g., regard for child perspectives,

sensitivity), classroom organization (e.g., behavioral guidance, engagement of children) and instructional supports used by teachers (e.g., quality of feedback, language modeling, concept development). Versions of the CLASS are available for toddler, preschool and early elementary classrooms, as well as for upper elementary and secondary classrooms.

The *Early Language and Literacy Classroom Observation*, or *ELLCO* (Smith & Dickinson, 2002) examines practices and environmental supports that encourage children's early literacy and language development in classrooms that serve children ages 3-8 (preschool to grade 3). The ELLCO includes a literacy environment checklist, an observation of classroom practices, and a teacher conference format for discussing findings.

---

34. Peterson, Valk, Baker, Brugger & Hightower, 2010.

Questions for Discussion

With a fellow mentor or other partner, choose a particular observation and assessment tool—preferably one that is used in your mentoring program—and practice articulating to each other the tool's rationales and goals; in particular, how the items are linked with children's learning. The purpose here is to practice helping your protégés become articulate on this subject, too.

You and your partner may wish to reflect on particular items on the assessment, and even on whether you agree with their underlying approach to teaching children. You might also consider whether some items will be universally applicable to all children. Are there any items, for example, that might be contraindicated for a child with special needs? Your goal here is not to reach "correct responses," but to ask questions, listen and gain a deeper understanding of the values that shape the assessment tools, as well as the values that shape your own approach to teaching.

READING AND RESEARCH

Another crucial area of mentoring is to model for your protégés how you as a teacher go about learning—how you investigate areas in which you want or need to know more. By doing so, you help develop a disposition of curiosity and inquiry, and offer your protégé the tools for continuing to learn and grow as a teacher on her own.[35] The central themes here are that:

- Teachers themselves are a rich source of information about teaching and learning;
- Teachers can actively construct and guide their own learning; and
- In-depth inquiry can lead to better ways to educate and care for young children.

Talk with each other about your "burning questions" related to teaching and learning. What do you wonder about? What classroom challenge(s) do you want to learn more about, and why? Why does this matter for the children?

To take one example: Consider a protégé who is bilingual in English and Tagalog, but has 18 children in her classroom who speak five different languages. She would like to know more about working in linguistically diverse classrooms, but has limited experience in this area. Discuss, together, the ways in which you will gather information, and what resources you will need. Perhaps you will visit other classrooms, interview teachers and parents, and/or make audio or video recordings of daily classroom interactions or activities. You will probably also find written resources on the subject, and do some reading and discussion together. Are there other ways for you to collect useful data?

Finally, analyze the information you have gathered. Compare your multiple sources of data, and reflect critically on your observation notes in order to interpret what children are doing, understanding and learning. Model for your protégé how to consider different perspectives, help her draw conclusions from her data, and encourage her to collect feedback from colleagues. Writing about her results can also help your protégé clarify her thinking, and sharing them with colleagues can help foster a collaborative learning community within the center.

Deepening your own knowledge as a mentor. There may be times when you are asked to work on an area in which you are relatively inexperienced, or when you need to get beyond your current teaching or problem-solving skills as a mentor. You may need deeper content knowledge and applied skills that relate to children's learning and teaching, depending on the design of your mentoring program or your protégés' backgrounds. By reading, talking with colleagues, accessing community resources, and/or developing a "research project" of your own, you may be able to expand your competencies sufficiently to meet your protégé's needs. But it is also appropriate to be candid if you don't think you have the knowledge or skills in a particular area that your protégé requires of you. If that is the case, consult with the leader of your mentoring program about whether there is another mentor who would be a better match for your protégé.

---

35. Meier & Henderson, 2007; Cochran-Smith & Lytle, 2001.

Mentor Feedback Form
(To be completed by the protégé)

Name of Mentor:

Name of Protégé:

Date:

Please use the following rating scale to evaluate your mentoring experience:
4 = Always 3 = Most of the time 2 = Sometimes 1 = Almost never

My mentor is sensitive to my learning and communication style. 4 3 2 1	Comments:
My mentor gives me helpful and specific feedback in a supportive way. 4 3 2 1	Comments:
My mentor helps me set reachable learning goals. 4 3 2 1	Comments:
My mentor provides or suggests useful resources and teaching tools. 4 3 2 1	Comments:
My mentor is dependable, and communicates with me in a timely fashion (by phone, by e-mail, in-person, etc.). 4 3 2 1	Comments:
My mentor is skilled at explaining how teaching strategies are related to children's learning. 4 3 2 1	Comments:
My mentor helps me establish routines and employ strategies that enhance my teaching and children's learning. 4 3 2 1	Comments:

What do you consider to be your mentor's strengths?

What areas do you think she needs to develop further?

Additional comments:

Mentor/Protégé Contact Log Template
(Can be completed by the mentor and/or by the protégé)

Date:
Start time:
End time:

Type of contact:
    ____ Face-to-face meeting
    ____ Telephone or Skype conversation
    ____ E-mail exchange
    ____ Text message exchange

Purpose of contact:
Summary of session/Issues explored:
Next steps:
Note: This page can be used for reporting purposes to the mentoring program, in order to track contact between the mentor and protégé. The mentor or protégé may also wish to add a second page of "Confidential Notes" for each contact, which would not be shared publicly.

TAKING STOCK OF PROGRESS

As you work together, you are helping your protégé to continually focus, revise, update and expand her goals. Periodically, as you come to the end of a cycle of observations and conferences, or after you have finished implementing a plan that you agreed upon in your contract, it will be time to look back at your earlier goals—taking stock of accomplishments, as well as any stalemates or conflicts—and perhaps set new goals, drawing up a revised mentor-protégé agreement about what you will do together in the next period of time. This is an important moment, too, for soliciting feedback from your protégé about your mentoring. (See the sample feedback form that follows.) You, or both of you, may also have feedback for the mentoring program itself. As you reach the end of one cycle, another cycle of growth and learning begins.

REFERENCES AND FURTHER READING

Bergen, S. (2009). *Best practices for training early childhood professionals.* St. Paul, MN: Redleaf Press.

Buysse, V. & Wesley, P. (2005). *Consultation in early childhood settings.* Baltimore: Brookes Publishing.

Cochran-Smith, M. & Lytle, S.L. (2001). Beyond certainty: Taking an inquiry stance. In Lieberman, A. & Miller, L., eds., *Teachers caught in the action.* New York: Teachers College Press.

Daloz, L. A. (1999). *Mentor: Guiding the journey of adult learners.* San Francisco: Jossey-Bass.

Garavuso, V. (2009). *Being mentored: Getting what you need.* New York: McGraw-Hill, Practical Guide Series.

Halle, T., Vick Whittaker, J. E. & Anderson, R. (2010). *Quality in early childhood care and education settings: A compendium of measures. Second edition.* Washington, DC: Child Trends. Prepared by Child Trends for the Office of Planning, Research and Evaluation, Administration for Children and Families, U.S. Department of Health and Human Services.

Harms, T., Clifford, R. M. & Cryer, D. (1998). *Early Childhood Environment Rating Scale Revised Edition (ECERS-R).* New York: Teachers College Press.

Harms, T., Cryer, D., & Clifford, R. M. (2003). *The Infant/Toddler Environment Rating Scale-Revised Edition (ITERS-R).* New York: Teachers College Press.

Harms, T., Cryer, D., & Clifford, R.M. (2007). *Family Child Care Environment Rating Scale Revised Edition (FCCERS-R).* New York: Teachers College Press.

La Paro, K., Hamre, B. & Pianta, R. (2012). *Classroom Assessment Scoring System™ (CLASS™) Manual, Toddler.* Baltimore: Brookes Publishing.

Meier, D. R. & Henderson, B. (2007). *Learning from young children in the classroom: The art and science of teacher research.* New York: Teachers College Press.

Peterson, S. M., Valk, C., Baker, A. C., Brugger, L. & Hightower, A. D. (2010). "We're not *just* interested in the work": Social and emotional aspects of early educator mentoring relationships. *Mentoring and Tutoring: Partnership in Learning, 18*(2), 155-175.

Pianta, R.C. (2003). *Standardized classroom observations from pre-K to third grade: A mechanism for improving quality classroom experiences during the P-3 years.* Baltimore: Brookes Publishing.

Pianta, R., La Paro, K. & Hamre, B. (2008). *Classroom Assessment Scoring System™ (CLASS™) Manual, K–3.* Baltimore: Brookes Publishing.

Roll, I., Aleven, V., McLaren, B.M. & Koedinger, K.R. 2007. Designing for metacognition: applying cognitive tutor principles to the tutoring of help seeking. *Metacognition and Learning,* 2(2): 125-140.

Schön, D, (1983). *The reflective practitioner: How professionals think in action.* New York: Basic Books.

Smith, M., & Dickinson, D. (2002). *Early Language and Literacy Classroom Observation (ELLCO) Toolkit,* Research Edition with User's Guide. Baltimore: Brookes Publishing.

Snow, C., & Van Hemel, S. (2008). *Early childhood assessment: Why, what and how? Report of the Committee on Developmental Outcomes and Assessments for Young Children.* Washington, DC: National Academies Press.

Stolovitch, H.D., & Keeps, E.J. (2011). *Telling ain't training,* Second edition. Alexandria, VA: American Society for Training and Development.

Takanishi, R. (1980). The unknown teacher: Symbolic and structural issues in teacher education. Keynote speech presented at the Midwest AEYC Conference, Milwaukee, WI, 1980.

Wiggins, G. (2012). Seven keys to effective feedback. In *Educational Leadership, 7(1),* 10-16.

Chapter 5

Mentors as Learners and Leaders

In this final chapter, we turn to other aspects of the mentoring role that are important to your success, whether you work with one or many protégés, or in conjunction with a school district, a college-based laboratory school, a quality improvement initiative, or another setting.

We begin by focusing on mentors as ongoing learners: the importance of continuing to develop your knowledge throughout your career, of identifying opportunities and relationships that can promote your professional growth over time, and of ensuring that your mentoring program supports your ongoing development and effectiveness. A number of states, as part of their early care and education workforce policies, have begun to articulate the competencies, qualifications, and preparation requirements that are appropriate for mentors.[36] Your mentoring program, ideally, will actively help you in developing strategies, and accessing resources, to address your learning needs in meeting such qualifications—often with the help of a coach or supervisor to guide your learning.

In the second part of the chapter, we focus on the role of mentors in the early care and education field as leaders and advocates who are uniquely equipped with close knowledge of the needs of teachers and providers.

MENTORS AS LEARNERS

In your role as a mentor, key parts of your job are to periodically assess your own knowledge and skills in relation to working with protégés, and to identify your ongoing learning goals. You can begin the process by thinking about what is going well in your work with your protégé, and what is challenging, by revisiting your responses to two activities we introduced in Chapter 1:

1. *What I Bring to the Mentoring Relationship:* In this activity, you were asked to rate your general competencies related to mentoring as adequately developed, somewhat developed, or not yet developed. If you have not yet strengthened your skills in one or more areas that you identified as in need of growth, these might be a good starting point for resetting your personal learning objectives. We urge you to redo this activity periodically, and to keep copies of it. Over time, it can provide a chronicle of your own professional growth and development—how you have changed, and how you have pursued different strategies for accomplishing your learning goals.

2. *Teaching Children and Mentoring Adults:* In this activity, you were asked to consider your skills related to teaching young children, as well as your ability to articulate the reasoning behind your teaching approaches. Depending on your mentoring program and the learning needs of your protégés, your needs to strengthen or articulate various aspects of teaching practice may change over time. A good practice is to reassess your content knowledge each time you work with a new protégé and/or if you change mentoring programs. If it feels appropriate, you might also consider sharing your self-assessment with your protégé, to emphasize the ongoing nature of your own learning.

---

36. U.S. Department of Health and Human Services, Administration for Children and Families, and Head Start Bureau, 2005; NAEYC & NACCRA, 2011.

 **Activity** Mentoring Knowledge and Skills Checklist

Organize your self-assessment with the use of the following checklist, which reflects all of the major topic areas covered in this book, listed by chapter.

I consider myself:	Very developed 1	Somewhat developed 2	Not yet developed 3
Chapter 2			
Knowledgeable about and able to apply theories of adult learning to my work as a mentor.			
Able to explain adult learning styles and apply them to my mentoring strategies.			
Skilled in assessing my protégé's stage of teacher development, and knowledgeable about what issues she may be concerned with during her particular stage.			
Chapter 3			
Well-versed in a range of communication strategies for working with my protégé.			
Skilled at building a trusting relationship with my protégé.			
Adept at problem-solving, in terms of arranging time and space to meet with my protégé.			
Knowledgeable about how culture can influence adult beliefs and practices about teaching and learning, and comfortable with asking and learning about my protégé's cultural traditions.			
Skilled at assessing my protégé's teaching practices, and identifying areas of strength and of potential improvement.			
Skilled at helping my protégé articulate her learning goals and the areas in which she would like to grow as a teacher.			
Able to balance my protégé's stated needs and goals with her stage of development and the goals of the mentoring program.			
Chapter 4			
Able to articulate my own teaching practices, and how they are related to children's learning.			
Skilled at providing specific, sensitive feedback in ways that are meaningful and manageable for my protégé.			
Able to draw from a wide range of mentoring strategies, and able to adjust these based on my protégé's needs.			
Able to offer my protégé support, as well as provide challenging learning activities to expand her teaching skills.			

Chapter 5			
Committed to my own ongoing learning and professional development.			
Comfortable with saying, "I don't know," and capable at researching further information on a variety of teaching issues with my protégé.			
Comfortable with soliciting feedback from my protégé about how well our work together is going.			
Familiar with any formal assessments that are used in my mentoring program, and able to articulate how these are connected to children's learning.			
Skilled at helping interpret the results of any such assessments with my protégé.			
Skilled at assessing the adult learning environment in my protégé's work setting.			

- What are your three greatest strengths related to mentoring knowledge and skills in the checklist above?
- Name three areas in which you would like to learn more in order to be a successful mentor.

Learning Environments for Mentors

As we discussed in Chapter 3, the quality of your protégé's teaching environment can greatly facilitate or impede her ongoing learning and the quality of her teaching practice. Similarly, for you as a mentor, the environment that your mentoring program creates for your work plays an important role in your ongoing development and effectiveness. Thinking about your own learning environment, and the impact it has on your work as a mentor, can help you become aware of how the environment can influence your protégé's teaching practice.

The Center for the Study of Child Care Employment at the University of California, Berkeley has developed an assessment tool—Supportive Environmental Quality Underlying Adult Learning (SEQUAL)—to study teaching and learning environments for adults in early care and education settings, based on an extensive review of research and theory about adult development, teacher education, organizational effectiveness, job satisfaction, and workplace stress.[37] The SEQUAL identifies five domains or dimensions of the environment that are necessary for effective teaching and teacher development, and that are just as important for mentors as they are for teachers of young children. These are:

1. Teaching Supports: features of the environment necessary for effective functioning.
2. Learning Community: support for adults' professional development.
3. Job Crafting: program policies that allow for and promote teacher initiative.
4. Adult Well-Being: program practices and policies that support adults' economic, physical and emotional needs.
5. Program Leadership: the role of supervisors and administrators in supporting staff.

---

37. Whitebook & Ryan, 2012.

The Center for the Study of Child Care Employment has also developed a version of the SEQUAL for mentors, the Mentor Learning Environment Checklist (SEQUAL-M), described in the following activity.

 **Activity** **Assessing Your Adult Learning Environment**

Assess your own adult learning environment with the following checklist. If you identify an area that needs improvement, explain how the status quo impedes your work. If you have difficulty thinking about how an area might be improved, your fellow mentors may be able to help you develop concrete suggestions or strategies for change. It's also helpful to think about who has the authority to make the changes you would like to see, and what information or approaches might garner their support.

THE MENTOR LEARNING ENVIRONMENT CHECKLIST

Learning Environment Domains	Rate as: Good, adequate, or in need of improvement	What specifically needs improvement?	Suggestions for improvement	Who has the authority to make the changes you seek?
Teaching Supports				
Well-delineated program goals and desired outcomes to guide your work with protégés				
Access to tools and strategies for assessing protégés' knowledge and skills, and how these change over time				
A program structure that assigns a manageable number of protégés to each mentor, and allows mentors sufficient opportunities to observe and meet with them				
Adequate workspace for meeting with protégés and performing other mentoring duties				
Access to resources, such as experts and support services, to assist you in working with protégés				
Learning Community				
Regular opportunities, such as a class, group meeting, or access to training, for learning and practicing your mentoring skills				

Learning Environment Domains	Rate as: Good, adequate, or in need of improvement	What specifically needs improvement?	Suggestions for improvement	Who has the authority to make the changes you seek?
A designated person (e.g., coach, coordinator, supervisor) to assist in preparing your professional development plan, including specific learning objectives and strategies for achieving them				
Opportunities for targeted learning for individual mentors				
An organized opportunity for professional sharing and reflection with other mentors about your experiences in working with protégés				
Job Crafting				
Clearly defined responsibilities and rules related to your work with protégés and their programs				
Authority to select or adapt mentoring strategies based on your assessment of protégés' learning needs				
Opportunities for input into policies and practices that influence the effectiveness and efficiency of your work				
Adult Well-Being				
Appropriate compensation and benefits				
Manageable workload for hours worked				
Fair and respectful working relationships				
Program Leadership				
Regular access to a supervisor or coordinator who:				
—is knowledgeable about teaching both children and adults				
—is familiar with your skills as a mentor				
—understands the challenges you face with protégés				
—is engaged in her own learning				
Additional Items You Consider Important				

After you have completed the Mentor Learning Environment Checklist, answer the following questions:

- For each item, describe how it could influence your work as a mentor.
- For those items you identified as needing improvement, explain how the current situation hinders your work as a mentor.
- Are there other items not mentioned above that you consider important to supporting good mentoring practice and ongoing learning?

Once you have answered these questions for yourself, share your ideas with other mentors. Do you agree on the essential features of a mentoring work environment that supports good practice and ongoing professional development? Are there any differences in perspective?

❓ Questions for Discussion

Both Mira and Aisha began mentoring other teachers without much prior experience of teaching young children. Over time, they have both become more aware of the mismatch between their knowledge and skills and their mentoring roles. Mira, for example, realizes that she had only begun to move beyond the survival stage of teaching during her brief period of preschool teaching, and finds herself short on instructional and classroom strategies, particularly when it comes to working with children whose behavior is challenging. After two years on the job, Aisha has spent time in many preschool classrooms, but considers some of her preschool-related competencies limited, and does not want to shortchange her protégés. Mira's program involves a biweekly, two-hour coaching meeting. Aisha's program brings mentors together quarterly for a half-day session.

- How might you advise Mira and Aisha to address their own learning needs?
- How does the structure of their mentoring programs ease or exacerbate their situations?
- Have you encountered similar problems yourself or among other mentors?
- What strategies have you used to support ongoing learning for yourself and fellow mentors?

MENTORS AS LEADERS

Ongoing concern about the quality of many early care and education services in the United States has led policymakers and other stakeholders to invest in improving the knowledge and skills of early educators, often by establishing or expanding mentoring programs. Mentors and coaches have become increasingly common in the early care and education workforce, with many seasoned teachers and providers aspiring to these roles.

As a mentor, you are uniquely situated at the intersection between the worlds of policy and practice. Most mentoring programs are designed in the service of quality improvement, and are supported with a blend of public and philanthropic dollars. Many mentoring programs undergo evaluation to determine how they can be improved and/or whether they should continue. As a mentor, you see the action close up, and thus your perspective on how protégés are faring is a very important one. You are positioned, for example, to assess how realistic the mentoring program's objectives are, based on protégés' stage of teacher development, how protégés' work environments impede or facilitate your efforts to help them improve their teaching, and, as discussed above, whether you are adequately supported in performing and improving in your role as a mentor.

For K-12 teachers, particularly during the first few years in the classroom, mentoring or coaching is viewed as essential to teacher preparation and development, and most states have implemented support programs for new teachers following the completion of their degrees or certification. In the early care and education world, qualifications and supports for teachers and providers vary by state, by program setting and by funding type, and while the availability of mentoring or coaching is expanding, such support is still not routinely available to teachers and providers working with children from birth to age 5.[38] Mentor leaders can help advocate for such programs, and can help ensure that they are well designed and include best practices to meet the needs of teachers and providers.

In all fields, a rewarding and supportive work environment is critical to attracting and retaining competent and dedicated employees. The early care and education profession is no different. Yet many ECE teachers work in environments that compensate them poorly, and receive little encouragement and support for continuing to build their professional skills. Many studies of early care and education programs have shown that various aspects of the work environment—such as high rates of teacher or director turnover, the absence of well-prepared co-workers, stress, and economic insecurity fueled by low pay—prevent teachers and programs from offering optimal care and instruction for young children.[39] Yet, too often, the workplace context of teaching young children—what teachers need in addition to training and education in order to succeed—receives minimal, if any, attention in professional development programs or quality improvement efforts in the ECE field.[40]

Mentors hold a unique perspective about protégés' learning environments, situated as they are at the nexus where children are taught and cared for, where teachers and providers are educated and trained, and where early education policy is made. Mentors can help bring the voices of those who work daily with children into the discussion of how to improve services for all young children, since children's well-being is directly linked to the well-being of their teachers.

We have explored the necessary elements of a good learning and working environment for you as a mentor. Next, by articulating what constitutes a supportive learning environment for your protégés, you can promote their understanding of how the work setting influences their practice. Mentors can support protégés to become articulate practitioners on their own behalf, and advocates for changes that can enable them to better meet the needs of children. The same five domains of your workplace learning environment—teaching supports, learning community, job crafting, adult well-being, and leadership—also influence your protégés' professional growth and teaching practice, although the items within each domain vary somewhat for the roles of mentor or teacher of young children. Each domain examines the policies, practices and relationships necessary for effective teaching.

To help you assess how well your protégé's workplace supports her in learning and growing as an effective teacher, the SEQUAL assessment tool may be useful in several ways.

38. Barnett, W.S., Carolan, M.E., Fitzgerald, J., & Squires, J.H. (2011). *The State of Preschool 2011: State Preschool Yearbook.* New Brunswick, NJ: National Institute for Early Education Research.
39. Helburn, 1995; Whitebook & Sakai, 2003; Whitebook & Sakai, 2004; Whitebook, Sakai, Gerber & Howes, 2001.
40. Whitebook & Ryan, 2011.

The following checklist adapted from the SEQUAL is designed to help you observe your protégé's work environment and gain an understanding of the degree to which it supports or impedes her teaching practice and growth. You can also use it as an educational tool with your protégé, talking with her, for example, about how the various items relate to children's learning and the ability to teach effectively, or asking her to reflect on particular items in her journal.

The full SEQUAL (available from CSCCE) is designed to be completed by all teaching staff in a given classroom or program, leading to an overall classroom or program rating. Some mentoring or coaching programs may administer the SEQUAL to determine a program's readiness to engage in a quality-improvement effort. If you are interested in asking protégés or programs to complete the full SEQUAL, this will require gaining permission both from your mentoring program and from the protégé's workplace.

Finally, as an educational and research tool, you can use the SEQUAL to familiarize a variety of early care and education stakeholders—such as directors, teacher educators, mentoring program coordinators, parents, policymakers and funding agencies—with concepts and best practices that teachers themselves identify as promoting their professional growth and development. In so doing, you can raise awareness about policies, practices and relationships in the early care and education workplace that foster good environments for young children. SEQUAL ratings can generate evidence linking good teaching with meeting teachers' needs, and will provide a basis for discussing how ECE programs can improve learning environments for teaching staff. The scenarios below illustrate different ways in which mentors can use the SEQUAL in their work.

Situation 1: Mira, a Quality Rating and Improvement System coach, uses the SEQUAL with her protégés to help them focus on how they work as a team. She uses the topics included in the SEQUAL, rather than the measure itself, and asks protégés to identify items they consider important to their ability to work well together to promote children's learning. Typically, she begins with one domain at a time, discussing others in subsequent meetings. She asks protégés to offer specific examples of the consequences of having, or not having, certain policies and practices in place. The process can also help build team spirit; her protégés are usually eager to discuss these issues, and have a lot to say. Sometimes, Mira chooses a specific SEQUAL item—for example, support for practicing new skills—and then asks protégés to assess their classroom in this regard, making suggestions for how they might do things differently.

Occasionally, the discussion can get heated, especially if protégés are discontented with particular aspects of their workplace environment. Depending on the program and issue, Mira might suggest that protégés talk to their union representative about how their concerns—for example, the amount of unpaid time it takes them to write up child assessments—might be addressed in their next contract. Or, depending on the program and the issue, Mira might help her protégés discuss how to talk with their director about it. For example, one group of protégés was being asked to read to small groups of children more frequently as part of their focus on literacy, but because of turnover, they no longer had a "floater" to help cover the rest of the classroom, since she had been assigned to another classroom full time. Talking it through with Mira, the protégés were able to agree to ask their director, at the next staff meeting, to come into the classroom more often until a permanent teacher was hired.

PROTÉGÉ LEARNING ENVIRONMENT CHECKLIST

Learning Environment Domains	Rate as: Good, adequate, or in need of improvement	What specifically needs improvement?	Suggestions for improvement	Who has the authority to make the changes you seek?
Teaching Supports				
Curriculum framework to guide teaching				
Appropriate and sufficient classroom materials				
Access to support services for children and families				
Sufficient numbers of trained staff at all times				
Established process for observing and assessing children's development				
Learning Community				
Individualized professional development plan in place for all teaching staff				
Opportunities for targeted individual professional development				
Opportunities for collaborative professional development				
Opportunities to share knowledge and skills with other teaching staff				
Support for practicing new skills				
Time to meet with classroom team to plan for children's learning				
Job Crafting				
Support for taking initiative				
Support for making decisions about teaching				
Input into center policies that affect teaching				
Adult Well-Being				
Adequate compensation and benefits				
Ergonomically safe physical environment and equipment				
Paid sick and vacation leave				
Fair and supportive work relationships				

PROTÉGÉ LEARNING ENVIRONMENT CHECKLIST (continued)

Learning Environment Domains	Rate as: Good, adequate, or in need of improvement	What specifically needs improvement?	Suggestions for improvement	Who has the authority to make the changes you seek?
Program Leadership				
Supervisors with knowledge of teaching and child development				
Supervisors familiar with protégé's practice and professional development needs				
Supervisors committed to creating time and opportunity for protégés to learn				

Adapted from the SEQUAL (Supportive Environmental Quality Underlying Adult Learning) assessment tool, Center for the Study of Child Care Employment, University of California, Berkeley

 Questions for Discussion

- Do you think Mira's approach to talking about the work environment is an effective way to approach team building?
- How might discussing your protégé's work environment with her facilitate your work?
- Do you think that your protégé's work environment promotes or hinders her learning?

Situation 2: Before a mentoring class, several of the mentors working in Aisha's program mention how stressed-out their protégés appear to be. Due to the state budget crisis, reimbursement rates have been reduced, and directors have laid off staff, reduced sick days, and cut back the substitute budget. Some protégés are working when ill, and others seem overwhelmed by classroom understaffing. The mentors find themselves stepping in to assist in the classrooms because they are concerned about the children's well-being. Several mentors approach their mentoring program coordinator to ask whether there is anything she can do. Brainstorming ideas with their coordinator, the mentors ask whether they could have their protégés fill out the economic well-being scale in the SEQUAL, and share the results at an upcoming state budget hearing or center board meeting. They are eager to make the case that quality improvement is impeded when the needs of teaching staff are not met. They also propose screening the work environment of early care and education centers before they are accepted to participate in the mentoring program, to ensure that they have the capacity to work on quality improvement. The mentoring program coordinator also suggests getting assistance for the directors whose programs are struggling, to help them manage their finances and perhaps find ways to restore some staffing prior to participating in the mentoring program.

- Have you ever raised issues about a protégé's work environment with your mentoring program coordinator? What was the issue? What was the outcome?
- If you haven't been called upon to be a spokesperson for your protégé, imagine a situation in which you are asked to talk to a policymaker about the needs of your protégés or other teachers.
- What advocacy skills did you use, or would you need, to be effective? Brainstorm with your fellow mentors about how you can build these skills.

* * * * * *

There is no single ingredient that leads to effective teaching. While mentoring is essential, it cannot entirely substitute for strong teacher education, or for good work environments that provide adequate teaching support, encourage teacher growth, and offer professional levels of compensation.

Yet mentors are in a unique position to serve not only as agents of change who help protégés improve their teaching practice and grow as professionals, but also as leaders and advocates who can contribute to broader improvements in adult work and learning environments in the field of early education. Mentors speak up about what teachers need for establishing warm and caring relationships with young children, tending the fires of children's curiosity and love of learning, and fostering their development and readiness for school.

This guide has been designed as a practical handbook to assist you in growing and developing as a mentor and leader—an articulate practitioner who combines knowledge of teaching young children with a broad range of skills for teaching and guiding adult learners. We hope this book will continue to be useful to you in your own professional commitment to lifelong learning, working as an agent of change on behalf of children and their teachers.

REFERENCES AND FURTHER READING

Barnett, W.S., Carolan, M.E., Fitzgerald, J., & Squires, J.H. (2011). *The State of Preschool 2011: State Preschool Yearbook.* New Brunswick, NJ: National Institute for Early Education Research.

Garavuso, V. (2009). *Being mentored: Getting what you need.* New York: McGraw-Hill, Practical Guide Series.

Helburn, S. W. (Ed.). (1995). *Cost, quality and child outcomes in child care centers. Technical report.* Denver: University of Colorado at Denver, Department of Economics, Center for Research in Economic and Social Policy.

Leana, C., Appelbaum, E. & Shevchuk, I. (2009). Work process and quality of care in early childhood education: The role of job crafting. *Academy of Management Journal*, 52 (6), 1169-1192.

Lower, J. K. & Cassidy, D. J. (2007). Child care work environments: The relationship with learning environments. *Journal of Research in Childhood Education*, 22(2), 189-204.

U.S. Department of Health and Human Services, Administration for Children and Families, and Head Start Bureau(2005). NAEYC & NACCRA, 2011.

Warren-Little, J. (2001). Professional development in pursuit of school reform. In A. Lieberman, & L. Miller (Eds.). *Teachers caught in the action: Professional development that matters*, pp. 23-44. New York: Teachers College Press.

Whitebook, M. & Ryan, S. (2011). Degrees in context: Asking the right questions about preparing skilled and effective teachers of young children, National Institute for Early Education Research, *Preschool Policy Brief* (22).

Whitebook, M & Ryan, S. (2012). *Supportive Environmental Quality Underlying Adult Learning (SEQUAL)*. Berkeley, CA: Center for the Study of Child Care Employment, University of California, Berkeley.

Whitebook, M. & Sakai, L. (2003). Turnover begets turnover: An examination of job and occupational instability among child care center staff. *Early Childhood Research Quarterly*, 18 (3), 271-395.

Whitebook, M. & Sakai, L. (2004). *By a thread: How child care centers hold on to teachers, how teachers build lasting careers*. Kalamazoo, MI: Upjohn Institute for Employment Research.

Whitebook, M., Sakai, L., Gerber, E. & Howes, C. (2001). *Then and now: Changes in child care staffing, 1994-2000*. Washington, DC: Center for the Child Care Workforce.

Wrzesniewski, A. & Dutton, J. E. (2001). Crafting a job: Re-envisioning employees as active crafters of their work. *Academy of Management Review*, 26, 179-201.

Zaslow, M., Tout, K., Halle, T., Whittaker, J. & Lavelle, B. (2010). Toward the identification of features of effective professional development for early childhood educators: Literature review. Washington, DC: Child Trends.

Supporting Teachers as Learners is a completely revised and expanded update of *The Early Childhood Mentoring Curriculum*, by Dan Bellm, Marcy Whitebook, and Patty Hnatiuk, published by the National Center for the Early Childhood Workforce (later the Center for the Child Care Workforce, American Federation of Teachers Educational Foundation) in 1997.

The authors would like to extend special thanks to the American Federation of Teachers for its generous support of this project. Many thanks as well to the readers and advisers who reviewed this book in earlier form, for their thoughtful and expert guidance: Lea Austin and Fran Kipnis of the Center for the Study of Child Care Employment, University of California, Berkeley; Vincent Costanza, early childhood program specialist, New Jersey Department of Education; Rory Darrah and Rosemarie Vardell, independent early care and education consultants; and the following members and staff of the American Federation of Teachers: Lisa Antonelli, Bill Harty, David Kammerer, Emilie Kudela, Debra Mahusky, Tish Olshefski, Carolyn Payton, Melissa Peterson, Brint Sagle, Jessica Smith, Megan Stockhausen, Cheryl Teare, Marla Ucelli-Kashyap, Teresa Valcarce and Julie Washington.